C0-DVF-679

Jesus'
Way

✠

Jesus' Way

✠

The 46-Day Lenten Journey
To Be Unconquerable in Christ

Devin Schadt

Excerpts from the English translation of the
Catechism of the Catholic Church, Second Edition,
©1994, 1997, 2000 by Libreria Editrice Vaticana,
United States Catholic Conference, Washington, D.C.
All rights reserved.

Unless otherwise noted,
Scripture quotations are from
the Douay-Rheims version of Sacred Scripture.
Copyright 1914 by John Murphy Company

Cover Design: Devin Schadt

© 2021 by Devin Schadt
All rights reserved.
Stewardship: A Mission of Faith
11 BlackHawk Lane
Elizabethtown, PA 17022
StewardshipMission.org

Printed in the United States of America

ISBN: 978-1-7358464-4-6

To David,

The Father's beloved; a son in the Son; a wounded healer;

a true follower of Christ who leads many to Christ;

a man whose heart burns with the fiery love of God;

a friend whose generosity knows no bounds,

Thank you.

Contents

"I am the way, and the truth, and the life. No man cometh to the father, but by me." John 14:6

"And I live, now not I; but Christ liveth in me." Galatians 2:20

"For let this mind be in you, which was also in Christ Jesus." Philippians 2:5

"Now this is eternal life: That they may know thee, the only true God, and Jesus Christ, whom thou hast sent." John 17:3

Jesus, particularly His human identity and His earthly pilgrimage as the Son of man, is the path we all must endeavor upon to attain the beatific vision, the Trinity.

To simplify this thought: Jesus is the person and path, particularly His human nature, to our destiny, the Trinity. For this reason, He calls Himself the Way: He, and His life's example, is the Way to eternal life in the Most Holy Trinity.

Introduction

This Lent Will Be Different

This Lent will be different.

How often have faithful Catholics made this hope-filled, courageous promise? Yet, by the second week of Lent, or third if we are strong, the harsh, humiliating reality of our pathetic fallen human nature trounces over that sacred idealistic pledge, leaving us discouraged, if not defeated. Year after year, truth be told, Lent— more or less—has the same results.

Easter comes. Easter goes. Like waves crashing upon the shores, so is this annual penitential season upon our souls. The relentless waves of those "forty days" do not demonstrate any significant change on the shoreline of our souls.

Days prior to Ash Wednesday, we tell ourselves and God that this will be the year that we will "do it right," that we will persevere to the bitter end and prove our love for Jesus. Yet, year after year, the season of Lent is no different, and, worse, we are no different. No significant, noticeable transformation has occurred. Which raises an important and clarifying question: What am I, or was I, supposed to change into?

Contained in the answer to this question is real, unlocked potential as to why this Lent can and will be different.

Though this penitential season involves certain renouncements, the essence of Lent is not about giving up certain consolations for the purpose of proving to ourselves and to God that we are finally making spiritual progress. Lent is not about giving up more but about being more, ironically, by realizing that we are less than God. It is not about giving up some things but becoming something—someone. Lent is about becoming the one thing that really, truly matters. The goal of Lent is to know Jesus, to follow His way, and to become like Him—to be another Christ—Christ unconquered.

Any other goal is pointless. The purpose of the Christian life is to become another Christ, *alter Christus*, to be able to confidently believe "it is no longer I who live, but Christ who lives in me" (Gal 2:20, ESV).

The reason our previous Lents have not changed is because we have not changed, and the reason we have not changed is because we have not changed our approach to Lent. The reason that we are not like Jesus is because we have not made that our goal.

The key to the spiritual life is identifying the correct target and shooting for it. If we choose an incorrect target, though we hit the bullseye consistently, we still miss the mark because we are aiming incorrectly.

Giving up chocolate, or booze, or coffee; taking on a new novena; exercising consistently; or attending daily Mass are good goals, but, in the end, they are not THE GOAL. And, if these "targets" don't help you hit the mark of becoming another Christ, they are not targets but diversions, regardless of how sacred they may appear to be.

How will this Lent be different? As Peter Kreeft wrote, "Sow a thought, reap an action; sow an action, reap a habit; sow a habit, reap a lifestyle; sow a lifestyle, reap a destiny."[1] To achieve our Christian destiny, which is exalted glorification in Christ, we must not only imitate Christ but live Christ's life. To live Christ's life, it

---

1   Peter Kreeft, *Prayer for Beginners* (San Francisco: Ignatius Press, 2000).

is necessary to develop habits like those of Jesus; to have habits like Jesus, it is imperative that we have specific daily practices that unite us with Christ; and to identify and fulfill those daily practices, we need to think with the mind of Christ.

If you are to become like Christ, it is crucial that you put on the mind of Christ (see Phil 2:5), that is, to think like Jesus. This is foundational to the spiritual life of a Christian. Often, we rely on our own ways and our own preset decisions, especially when it comes to Lent and the spiritual life. But beware, His ways are far above our ways (see Is 55:9). This Lenten journey with Christ will challenge you to think much differently. Only by thinking with the mind of Christ, can we begin to live Jesus' way.

THE PURPOSE OF JESUS' WAY

The singular purpose of *Jesus' Way* is to learn and live Jesus Christ's spirituality—His way of life—not only during Lent but for the remainder of our lives on earth. To accomplish this, *Jesus' Way* provides rich daily reflections that will allow you to think with the mind of Christ and spiritual practices that will help you live with the heart of Christ. In other words, when Lent ends, your new way of life in Jesus will only be beginning. On Easter Sunday, you will truly rise in Christ to a new way of life—Jesus' life.

WHY 46 DAYS

The Lord Jesus, upon His triumphal entry into Jerusalem, entered the Temple that had become overrun and occupied by money changers and those selling overpriced oxen, sheep, and doves to pilgrims for their sacrificial offerings. After Jesus made a whip of cords, turned over the money tables, and drove those usurpers from His Father's house, the Jews demanded that He demonstrate by what authority He had the right to do this. Jesus responded by saying, "Destroy this temple, and in three days I will raise it up" (Jn 2:19).

"The Jews then said: Six and forty years was this temple in building; and wilt thou raise it up in three days?" (Jn 2:20).

The forty-six years that it took for the Jews to build the Temple is a symbol of the forty-six days of Lent (including Sundays), in which we attempt to build the Lord's temple by our penitential habits. But, like the Jews, we can miss the target. Christ's Temple, His body, was the real place of worship, while Herod's Temple was a sign intended to point people to that reality. We can often be so focused on building our own temple that we neglect to participate in Jesus' action of building His temple in us.

The forty-six days of Lent is a symbol of man's efforts to build a temple for Christ. Yet, we forget that it is Christ, ultimately, who builds the temple in us. In other words, our focus should not be on building ourselves, but rather our focus should be on Christ who does the building. We are not to establish our own way but rather follow Jesus' way.

The purpose of this Lenten devotional is to move us from self-reliance, which always leads to self-hatred, to being completely dependent on Jesus, allowing Him to make us His holy temples—His dwelling place. However, this can only occur if we are humble, and humility most often comes by means of humiliations. The purpose of Lent and its forty-six days is to demonstrate to us that we are incapable of building the temple of God in ourselves—only God can; yet, God demands our participation in that divine work.

This Lent will be different because you will cease to base the success of this season on whether you failed to fulfill your penitential commitments. This Lent will be different because it is precisely amidst those failures that you will come to know Christ and understand that He has stood in your place and ransomed you from your sins, and that only by following Him will He give you the power to be like Him.

Peter denied Jesus. The Apostles abandoned Jesus. Judas betrayed Jesus. Yet, for those who returned to Christ and trusted in His mercy, Jesus imparted to them the power to be like Him. This Lent you will come to realize that your relationship with God is not performance based. Jesus simply wants you to become Him, so that nothing, not even your failures, can conquer your confidence in Him.

This Lent will be different because *you* will not build the temple, but rather Christ will build His temple in you. You will not focus on yourself, but rather you will focus on Christ who dwells within you. The goal of Lent is to become like Christ by knowing Christ, and we do this by following Jesus' way.

THE STRUCTURE OF *JESUS' WAY*

Jesus' Way invites you, over the course of forty-six days, to journey with Christ from His baptism to His final moments on the Cross. Comprised of seven stages, each having its own daily reflections and spiritual practices, *Jesus' Way* will help you not only to know about Jesus but practically embrace and live the life of Jesus Christ. By learning who Jesus really is, you will come to embrace and live His holy way, and, by living His holy way, you will come to experience His divine love—and this love is transformative.

At each stage, two or three spiritual practices are selected and continued throughout the Lenten journey. In other words, the spiritual practices of each stage compile with the previous stage's practices so that, by the end of your Lenten journey, you will have an ongoing spiritual blueprint for your life.

The spiritual practices are specifically designed to help you cultivate a rich, consistent, vibrant prayer life, to be more generous and courageous with your almsgiving and sacrificial offerings, and to love those who you may deem unlovable and to forgive those who you may believe to be unforgivable, including yourself. *Jesus' Way*, if embraced, will allow you the incredible opportunity to die to yourself with Jesus, and, therefore, to be raised up by God our Father with Jesus.

Jesus promises that He is the way, the truth, and the life (see Jn 14:6), and only by Him and His way may we come to God our Father. May *Jesus' Way* become your way—your way to discovering yourself in Christ and Christ in you—that you may know that you are a son of God in God the Son and live in that unconquerable truth.

SPIRITUAL PRACTICES

Stage 1: Identity and Mission in Christ

The purpose of this stage is to discover Christ's identity, to discover our identity in Christ, and to have His image burned into us that we may become revelations of His eternal glory.

- Tape an image of the Holy Face of Jesus to your bathroom mirror (Included on page 301). When in front of it, pray: "Lord Jesus burn the image of your holy face into me that I may become a revelation of your glory, that I may proclaim as did the holy Apostle: *"It is no longer I who live, but Christ who lives in me"* (Gal 2:20, ESV, emphasis added).

Stage 2: Calling and Cleansing

The purpose of this stage is to avail ourselves to be cleansed by Christ so that He may abide in the temple that we are. To accomplish this, we increase our ability to discern the Lord's direction and counsel by developing a consistent, intimate, morning prayer routine.

- Pray the morning offering.
- Meditate on the daily Gospel—the 7 R's of prayer.
- Pray a Scriptural Rosary decade(s).
- Practice 15 minutes of prayer / 5 minutes of silence (using *The Liturgy of Hours* or Sacred Scripture as a basis for prayer).

Stage 3: Precepts and Preparation

The purpose of this stage is to increase our ability to discern the Lord's direction and counsel and identify those habits and sins that are contrary to Christ so that we may repent of them. This is accomplished primarily by frequent examination of conscience and Confession and by developing a consistent and intimate evening prayer.

- Make an examination of conscience.
- Practice 15 minutes of prayer / 5 minutes silence (using *The Liturgy of Hours* or Sacred Scripture as a basis for prayer).
- Pray a Scriptural Rosary decade(s).
- Practice spiritual reading.
- Go to weekly Confession.

Stage 4: *Summons to Sacrificial Responsibility*

The purpose of this stage is to develop a spirit of sacrifice that fosters a sense of courage and increases our capacity to become responsible for those who are entrusted to us. Prayer becomes powerful when supported and animated by sacrifice. Only a leader who sacrifices himself and his selfish will is worthy of being followed.

- Make one daily hidden sacrifice.
- Reduce all forms of social media.
- Give up your phone during family time.
- Do not look at the phone, emails, social media, or news until after morning prayer.
- Do not look at the phone, emails, social media, or news after evening prayer.
- Limit yourself to one movie or television program per week.
- Do not listen to music or news while in the car.

Stage 5: *Communion and Companionship with Christ*

The purpose of this stage is to cultivate a true, profound devotion to our Lord in the Most Blessed Sacrament of the Altar, loving and worshipping Him in the Eucharist by means of watches, frequent reception of Holy Communion, and litanies of thanksgiving,

- Attend one extra Holy Mass per week (in addition to Sunday).
- Make at least one Holy Hour or add an extra Holy Hour per week.
- Develop a personal litany of thanksgiving to be recited while present before the Most Blessed Sacrament.

Stage 6: Testimony and Trials

The purpose of this stage is to develop a generous heart in the image of Jesus' Sacred Heart. Jesus surrendered all that He possessed so that we may possess Him and His life. Therefore, we identify ways to be more generous to our neighbors and fellow man, particularly those who have great needs. Truly, the one who gives begins to live.

- Make one larger charitable donation to a mission or institution that works with the less fortunate.
- Visit an elderly, sick, or homebound person.
- Devote time to assisting someone with a project.
- Ensure that you tithe (10%) to your local parish (the tithe should be based on gross income).

Stage 7: Love and Legacy

By overcoming all bitterness, resentment, and lack of forgiveness lodged secretly deep in our hearts, this stage affords us the opportunity to imitate Christ who said from the Cross, "Father, forgive them, for they know not what they do" (Lk 23:34). By forgiving as Christ forgives, we will find our freedom in Him.

- Forgive someone who has betrayed, offended, or wounded you by asking God to bless them daily.
- Ask forgiveness, in person, by phone, or by letter from someone whom you have injured, offended, wounded, or betrayed.
- Praise and thank God specifically for the talents and gifts that you are jealous or envious of in a certain individual.

- Intentionally pray for God's blessing and salvation for an enemy or someone you dislike or find disagreeable.
- Forgive yourself, believing that God has forgiven you (for you are to love your neighbor as yourself).

Stage 1

Ash Wednesday to First Saturday of Lent

IDENTITY AND MISSION IN CHRIST

During this preparatory stage of our Lenten journey, we encounter Jesus as He commences His most sacred mission. Over the course of the following four days, Our Lord reveals to us precisely what pleases God our Father, the two foundational principles of the Christian man's spiritual life: identity and mission, and the rite of passage—an intense fire of testing and temptation—which is essential if one is to endure the spiritual combat. Our chief concern is to avail ourselves to the Holy Spirit that the image of Jesus may be burned into us—that we may more fully assume the identity of Christ and that His life be lived in and through us—so that we may, with the holy Apostle, confidently proclaim: *It is no longer I who live, but Christ who lives in me* (see Gal 2:20, ESV, emphasis added). By means of the practice of gazing with devotion upon the sacred image of Jesus' Holy Face, we avail ourselves to become a living reflection of His divine countenance.

STAGE 1 SPIRITUAL PRACTICES

The purpose of this stage is to discover Christ's identity, to discover our identity in Christ, and to have His image burned into us that we may become revelations of His eternal glory.

Tape an image of the Holy Face of Jesus to your bathroom mirror. When in front of it, pray: "Lord Jesus, burn the image of your holy face into me that I may become a revelation of your glory, that I may proclaim as did the holy Apostle, *It is no longer I who lives but Christ who lives in me* (see Gal 2:20, ESV, emphasis added).

Day 1

(Preparation Week: Ash Wednesday)

INVOCATION: JESUS, GRANT ME THE GRACE TO PLEASE GOD THE FATHER.

THE FOUNDATION OF THE SPIRITUAL LIFE: PLEASING GOD

The Baptism of Our Lord

"Thou art my beloved Son;
in thee I am well pleased." Mark 1:11

The single principle upon which the Christian's spiritual life is founded is knowing and doing that which pleases God. Knowledge without action is neglect, and action without knowledge is presumption. "Knowledge puffeth up; but charity edifieth" (1 Cor 8:1). Love of God is *doing* what pleases Him by *knowing* what pleases Him.

If a man desires to be holy, it is imperative that he look to and learn from Jesus, who said, "He that sent me, is with me, and he hath not left me alone: for I do always the things that *please him*" (Jn 8:29, emphasis added).

What *things* then does Jesus *always* do that please His Father? By returning to the first recorded scriptural account, wherein God expresses His pleasure in Jesus, we discover two foundational principles necessary if we are to please God. As Christ was baptized by John the Baptist, while rising from the waters of the Jordan, the heavens thundered with God the Father's solemn pronouncement, His approval and confirmation, "Thou art my beloved Son; in thee I am well pleased" (Mk 1:11). This raises a question: Why was God the Father pleased with Jesus? At this point in the life of Christ, He had not performed any public miracles, nor had He accomplished any works that would be perceived as astounding or stupendous. Indeed, Jesus had, up to this point, lived in obscurity, serving His parents inconspicuously in their humble Nazarene home.

God the Father expressed His pleasure with His Son precisely because Jesus is His only beloved Son. Jesus is God's own; this is His identity. As a father loves his child, not because of any grand achievements, but simply because the child is *his* child, so also God the Father loves His Son because He is His Son. The first principle of pleasing God is for a man to believe that God is his Father and that he is God's adopted son, and to know and believe that this is his identity. This filial belief enables a man to please God not by his works but by faith, which is to trust in the Father.

Notice also that God the Father expresses His delight with Jesus, His Son, precisely after He is baptized. This indicates that God is pleased with us not because of what we have done, or are capable of doing, but because of what He has done for us. Being baptized in Christ, God justifies us in His sight without any merit of our own and makes us His adopted sons.

Furthermore, God the Father is also pleased with Jesus because Jesus is certain of His identity as God's Son and certain of His Father's love for Him. This filial confidence in His Father compels Jesus to profess, "I receive glory not from men" (Jn 5:41). Notice that Jesus does not depend upon worldly glory or status to determine his value and identity, but rather He knows and trusts that He is the Father's own and that His Father will glorify Him. The second principle of pleasing God is to not seek glory from men, nor to desire to glorify oneself, but to seek only to glorify God the Father.

As the Apostle says, "Let this mind be in you, which was also in Christ Jesus: Who being in the form of God, thought it not robbery to be equal with God: But emptied himself, taking the form of a servant, being made in the likeness of men. . . . He humbled himself, becoming obedient unto death, even to the death of the cross" (Phil 2:5–8).

The word rendered as "form" is the technical Greek word *morphé*, which means an outward expression that embodies an essential inner substance—a permanent essence. This indicates that, though Jesus is God the immutable Word, He deprived Himself of the glorified status associated with His divinity. In other words, Jesus emptied Himself of exaltation as a sign and lesson to every man that God is most pleased when we detach ourselves from the desire of obtaining human honor or grasping for a noble status. The Christian man concerns himself not with glorifying himself, for he is certain that, by glorifying his Creator, God will glorify the creature.

The two fundamental reasons for God taking pleasure in His Son—knowledge of His identity as God's only Son and total trust in God so as to not look for glory from men—are intimately connected and dependent upon the other. The former is based on *being*, while the latter is discovered in *doing* that which the Son of God does.

To empty oneself of the pursuit of self-exaltation, a man must be resolutely confident in his identity as a son of God, while also believing with absolute certainty that God is his *Abba* to such a degree that he refuses to succumb to seeking glory for himself. Indeed, he deliberately chooses not to glorify himself for he has faith that God will share with him His glory.

To become like Christ, we must have the mind of Christ who, because of His filial confidence, emptied Himself, depriving Himself of status and glory, and became the servant of all. Indeed, "whatsoever you do, do it from the heart, as to the Lord, and not to men" (Col 3:23), "not serving to the eye, as pleasing men, but in simplicity of heart, fearing God" (Col 3:22). This is the foundation of the spiritual life.

Lord Jesus, burn the image of your holy face into me
that I may become a revelation of your glory,
that I may proclaim as did the holy Apostle:
"It is no longer I who live, but Christ who lives in me."[2] *Amen.*

Optional Scripture Readings: Mark 1:1–11; Philippians 2:6–8

FULFILL YOUR SELECTED SPIRITUAL PRACTICES FROM STAGE 1:
IDENTITY AND MISSION IN CHRIST.

---

2   Galatians 2:20, emphasis added; this verse, which occurs at the end of each day, is from the English Standard Version (ESV) of the Bible.

Day 2

(Preparation Week)

INVOCATION: JESUS, REVEAL TO ME MY SACRED MISSION.

THE SPIRITUAL LIFE'S SACRED MISSION

The Baptism of Our Lord – Continued

———

"Behold the Lamb of God." John 1:29

The two fundamental arms of the Christian man's life are identity and mission. So interdependent upon one another are these two that to neglect one would be to neglect the other. For if a man knows not who he is, how can he know who he is to become? If a man does not comprehend his identity in Christ as a son of God, how can he become like God's Son, the Christ? Unaware of his identity, he lacks a real sense of mission, never achieving his destiny. Unaware of his destiny, he fails to undertake the mission demanded and dependent upon his identity. Yet, by becoming more aware of who we are in Christ, we can receive the grace to become like Christ the Son.

Following Jesus' baptism, after hearing God the Father's solemn pronouncement, John the Baptist cried aloud, "Behold the Lamb of God" (Jn 1:29). God proclaims His Son's identity, while man announces God the Son's mission—He is to be the Lamb of God.

Threaded throughout Israel's salvation history is the reoccurring theme of the "Lamb of God." Abraham, commanded by God to
sacrifice Isaac his son, his only son whom he loved (see Gen 22:2), is
asked by Isaac as they climbed Mount Moriah, "Behold . . . fire and
wood: where is the victim for the holocaust?" (Gen 22:7). To which
Abraham responded, "God will provide himself a victim" (Gen 22:8).

When the angel of God demanded that Abraham spare his son,
the Scripture says, "Abraham lifted up his eyes, and saw behind his
back a ram amongst the briers sticking fast by the horns, which he
took and offered for a holocaust instead of his son" (Gen 22:13). The
lamb which God would provide had not yet been provided by God.

Approximately four centuries later, to manifest His power, and
to liberate the Israelites from being enslaved by the Egyptians, God
inflicted the Egyptians with the culminating tenth plague—the death
of the firstborn (see Ex 11:1–12:36). God, through Moses, commanded
that every Israelite family procure a lamb "without blemish, a male,
of one year: according to which rite also you shall take a kid" (Ex
12:5) and sacrifice the lamb, mark the doorposts and lintels of their
dwellings with its blood (see Ex 12:7), and "eat the flesh that night
roasted at the fire, and unleavened bread with wild lettuce" (Ex 12:8).

"And it came to pass at midnight, the Lord slew every firstborn
in the land of Egypt, from the firstborn of [Pharaoh], who sat on
his throne, unto the firstborn of the captive woman that was in the
prison, and all the firstborn of cattle" (Ex 12:29), while the angel of
death "passed over" the Israelites.

By means of the figure and symbol of the lamb, God established
a profound correlation between the lamb and the firstborn son. The
lamb was the object of sacrifice that enabled the son, an object of
affection, to be ransomed.

+ JMJ +

From Moses to Christ, over the course of the centuries, millions upon millions of lambs were sacrificed as a remembrance that God had spared His firstborn son, Israel, from slavery to Egypt and slavery to the sin of idolatry.

Nevertheless, Israel's iniquity became so foul and depraved that an infinite number of sacrificial lambs could not cover the multitude of its sins. Israel was beyond ransom. Indeed, "all we like sheep have gone astray, every one hath turned aside into his own way" (Is 53:6).

Yet, at the fullness of time, the true Lamb of God, the one who would take upon Himself the sins of the world (see Jn 1:29), was revealed: "And beholding Jesus walking, [John the Baptist] saith: Behold the Lamb of God" (Jn 1:36).

From all eternity it was God the Son's will, in union with His Father, to fulfill the mission to be the Lamb of God upon whom the iniquity and the sin of mankind fell. The mission of the Lamb of God was to sacrifice Himself for our transgressions: "And the Lord hath laid on him the iniquity of us all. He was offered *because it was his own will*" (Is 53:6–7, emphasis added).

In the person of Jesus, the Lamb and the Son become one. He is the unblemished (sinless), male, sacrificial Lamb whose mission is to make atonement for men, but, as in the first Passover, we must partake of the Lamb's flesh.

It is not satisfactory nor sufficient for us to express our gratitude with our lips, but we must do so with our lives. Indeed, the praise that passes over our lips must be professed by our deeds. As the psalmist asks: "What shall I render to the Lord, for all the things he hath rendered to me?" (Ps 116:12). "I will pay my vows to the Lord before all his people: precious in the sight of the Lord is the death of his saints" (Ps 116:14–15).

In other words, Christ's mission is not His exclusively; it also is

31

the mission of the Christian. Indeed, Jesus' sacrifice has won for us the grace and honor to sacrifice for Jesus. We have the privilege to participate in His sacrifice by offering our "bodies a living sacrifice, holy, pleasing unto God, your reasonable service" (Rom 12:1)—this is your true and proper worship. Indeed, it is our privilege "not only to believe in him, but also to suffer for him" (Phil 1:29). For this reason, St. Paul can conclude that "for [his] sake we are put to death all the day long. We are accounted as sheep for the slaughter" (Rom 8:36).

It is a great paradox that to be privileged in Christ is to become a sacrificial lamb. If a man be a true son of God, he is to become another lamb of God. The mission of a son of God is to be one with the Lamb of God and His mission. By means of your self-sacrifice, in union with Christ's sacrifice, you will become capable of transmitting God's divine life to others. This is your mission. "For unto this are you called: because Christ also suffered for us, leaving you an example that you should follow his steps" (1 Pt 2:21).

Lord Jesus, burn the image of your holy face into me
that I may become a revelation of your glory,
that I may proclaim as did the holy Apostle.
"It is no longer I who live, but Christ who lives in me." Amen.

Optional Scripture Readings: John 1:19–37; Exodus 11:1–12:36

FULFILL YOUR SELECTED SPIRITUAL PRACTICES FROM STAGE 1:
IDENTITY AND MISSION IN CHRIST.

Day 3

(Preparation Week)

INVOCATION: JESUS, TEACH ME HOW TO DECREASE
THAT YOU MAY INCREASE IN ME.

THE CHRISTIAN MAN'S ETHOS

The Baptism of Our Lord – Continued

"He must increase, but I must decrease." John 3:30

If a man be full of himself, there is little, if any, room within himself for God. The grasping for self-exaltation will certainly end with grave humiliation. If you desire glory, pursue and embrace humility. The sure way to be filled with God's spirit is to empty oneself of the spirit of pride.

Determined to know John the Baptist's identity, the anxious Jews sought him in the desert and asked if he was the Christ, to which he responded, "I am not the Christ, but that I am sent before him" (Jn 3:28). Therefore, he concludes, "He must increase, but I must decrease" (Jn 3:30).

John was the voice who directed his followers to the Word. The Baptist was a lamp shining on the true Light. John the creature glorifies Christ his creator.

We should take our lesson from John the Baptist. He is thought to be like Christ; he declares he is not what they think. He does not take advantage of their mistake to further his own glory. . . . He saw where his salvation lay. He understood that he was a lamp, and his fear was that it might be blown out by the wind of pride.[3]

Many the disciple who falls into the trap of serving his Lord for the purpose of usurping His glory, loving the Giver for only the sake of His gifts. Is this not the essence of the original sin—to be like God without God?

Man desires significance. The modern definition of significance is to be worthy of attention, importance. Worldly significance is always dependent upon deriving value from others. When a man becomes attached to this type of significance, he exchanges his true identity for fallen man's external perception of him. The Latin word for significance, *significare,* is comprised of the two Latin root words *signe* (sign) and *facare* (to make). True significance is derived from being a sign that directs humanity to a transcendental reality—God. Rather than basing one's identity on external perception, true significance is an internal identity that signifies an external, greater reality.

The purpose of the Christian life is to be transformed into a sign that directs humanity beyond itself to the reality of God. Paradoxically, when the Christian man directs people to Christ and not himself, he becomes like John. In fact, John so closely resembled Christ that the Jews mistook him for the Christ. John, however, did not usurp Jesus' glory as his own, and, because of this, God glorified John with the crown of sanctity. John emptied himself that we may know Christ, and Christ emptied Himself that we may be filled with God (see Phil 2:7).

3   St. Augustine; *Sermo,* 295.

As the moon reflects the light of the sun into the darkness of night, so a son of God uses the light and glory he has received from God to reveal the glory of God. When the moon, however, is positioned between the sun and the earth, it eclipses the sun's light, veiling the world in darkness. When a man intentionally attempts to gain the attention, focus, and accolades of others, he eclipses the very light of the Son of God. He forgets that the light he reflects is not his own but belongs solely to God.

If you are to be a man who is not bound by worldly significance or enslaved by human perception, it is necessary that you have the ethos of John and decrease that Jesus may increase in and through you. Confess to yourself often, "I am not the Christ," and, in doing so, you will begin to reflect Christ and direct others to Him.

Therefore, humble yourself under the mighty hand of God and, in due time, He will exalt you (see 1 Pt 5:6).

Lord Jesus, burn the image of your holy face into me
that I may become a revelation of your glory,
that I may proclaim as did the holy Apostle:
"It is no longer I who live, but Christ who lives in me." Amen.

Optional Scripture Readings: John 3:26–30

FULFILL YOUR SELECTED SPIRITUAL PRACTICES FROM STAGE 1:
IDENTITY AND MISSION IN CHRIST.

Day 4

(Preparation Week)

INVOCATION: JESUS, HELP ME TO EMBRACE
MY TRUE IDENTITY IN YOU.

THE CHRISTIAN MAN'S IDENTITY TESTED

Jesus Is Driven by the Holy Spirit into the Wilderness

"And immediately the Spirit drove [Jesus]
out into the desert." Mark 1:12

It is a perplexing paradox that temptation is a means to salvation, for, if a man encounters temptation and rises above it, he has proved his love for and increased his capacity to love God. Overcoming temptation is a proof of love for only love animated by faith can overcome temptation truly, and faith is demanded of the one who is being tested.

"Truly I tell you that no one should consider himself a perfect friend of God until he has passed through many temptations and tribulations."[4] Indeed, the one who taught His disciples to pray

---

4   St. Francis of Assisi, Jill Haak Adels, *Wisdom of the Saints*, Barnes & Noble Books, 1987, p151.

"[Father] lead us not into temptation" (Mt 6:13) was led by the Holy Spirit into temptation (see Mt 4:1).

Promptly after His baptism and His Father's pronouncement of His identity, Jesus was driven by the Holy Spirit into the wilderness to be tested. To understand Jesus, and ourselves, it is imperative that we understand fundamentally the essence of Christ's temptation. By understanding Jesus' intended purpose for entering the forty-day trial in the wilderness, we will penetrate with precision the essence of His temptation and how His temptation is every man's test.

Recall that God claimed Israel as His firstborn son. This firstborn son, however, while flourishing in the land of Egypt, fell prey to the worship of Egyptian gods, and, as a consequence, eventually became enslaved by Pharaoh himself.

Through God's chosen servant Moses, God commanded Israel to break their physical and spiritual fetters and flee from Egypt into the desert. As Scripture says, "Israel was a child, and I loved him: and I called my son out of Egypt" (Hos 11:1). While wandering for forty years in the desert, God tested the Israelites to determine whether they would remain the slave or become the son.

Over the course of their desert wanderings, Israel failed the test miserably, specifically on three occasions: first, the children of Israel grumbled against God for not having bread to eat; second, when Moses tarried on Mount Sinai for the length of forty days, the Israelites began to believe him to be dead and, therefore, crafted for themselves a golden calf, which they worshipped; third, they rebelled against Moses, complaining bitterly that they were without water, and, therefore, Moses vented his frustration by striking the rock that God had commanded him to strike—

not once—but twice. Though water did flow from the rock, as God had promised, God punished Moses for his lack of patience, denying him the joy of entering the Promised Land before the completion of his days.

Jesus, God's firstborn Son, entered the desert with the intention to redeem and reclaim for Israel the divine sonship that Israel had squandered. Jesus is the typological fulfillment of Israel, as noted by St. Matthew, who references the event of St. Joseph taking the Christ child and His Mother and fleeing from Herod to Egypt: "That it might be fulfilled which the Lord spoke by the prophet, saying: Out of Egypt have I called my son" (Mt 2:15). Again, Jesus remained in the wilderness for forty days and forty nights as a typological fulfillment of Israel's forty-year wandering in the desert.

During this forty-day period, the devil assaulted Jesus with three temptations: "If thou be the Son of God, command that these stones be made bread" (Mt 4:3); "Again the devil took [Jesus] up into a very high mountain, and shewed him all the kingdoms of the world, and the glory of them, And said to him: All these will I give thee, if falling down thou wilt adore me" (Mt 4:8–9); and again the devil tempted Jesus saying, "If thou be the Son of God, cast thyself down, for it is written: That he hath given his angels charge over thee, and in their hands shall they bear thee up, lest perhaps thou dash thy foot against a stone" (Mt 4:6).

Each of these three temptations is specifically aimed at attacking Jesus' identity as the Son of God. Initially, it may appear that Satan was asking Jesus merely to reveal His true identity. However, probing deeper into the scriptural account, we discover that the devil was attempting to plant into the heart of Jesus a seed of doubt that God is not His Father or, at the very least, that God is not a

Father who can be trusted. Trust, the essence of sonship, was and is precisely what the devil endeavors to undermine.

The question, "Are you the Son of God?" is another way of asking, "Is God really your Father?" "Does God really love you?" "Will God share with you His power?" "Prove it." "Do these miracles, or bow down to me, and I will give you the power and validation that your Father won't give."

The fundamental core of every temptation is an attack on God's fatherhood, His goodness, and our trust in and fidelity to Him. All temptation ultimately is an assault on our filial relationship with God the Father. How a man responds to this temptation determines whether he remains a slave to the devil or becomes a trusting son of God.

Because of his lack of faith, the slave bows down to the devil, seeking disordered validation from the world, and endeavors to prove to the world that he is chosen, important, and needed.

On the other hand, the son, like Jesus, trusts in God the Father's benevolence. A true son of God derives confidence, assurance, and strength from God his Father, knowing with certainty that he is His son. Therefore, he does not bow down to the world's evaluation of him, for God's approval is sufficient.

Therefore, be aware my son, every test and temptation that you will undergo determines whether you will be a slave of the world and the devil or if you will become a faithful son of the Father. It is impossible that temptations will not come; therefore, it is vital that we learn to leverage them to our advantage by overcoming them.

Lord Jesus, burn the image of your holy face into me
that I may become a revelation of your glory,
that I may proclaim as did the holy Apostle:
"It is no longer I who live, but Christ who lives in me." Amen.

Optional Scripture Readings: Mark 1:12–13; Matthew 4:1–11

FULFILL YOUR SELECTED SPIRITUAL PRACTICES FROM STAGE 1:
IDENTITY AND MISSION IN CHRIST.

Stage 2

First Week of Lent
Calling and Cleansing

During this second stage of our Lenten journey, we receive Jesus' summons to follow Him and become His disciples. As we receive His yoke, that is, His divine teaching, and heed His call, He discloses the essentials of the spiritual life: listening to the Word, obedience to the Word we have received, a resolute commitment to taking upon oneself the Cross, and the pure motivation of doing so solely for the glory of Almighty God. During the following seven days, Jesus reveals His ardent desire to enter and dwell within your sacred temple, but, to accomplish this, it is imperative that this temple be cleansed of all idols that haunt and occupy your soul. Once cleansed, Jesus applies the tender mercy needed for you to be a living expression of His salvation. By means of developing a consistent, attentive morning prayer routine, we avail ourselves to the practice of listening and discerning the still small voice of God.

Stage 2 Spiritual Practices
(select two or three)

The purpose of this stage is to avail ourselves to be cleansed by Christ so that He may abide in the temple that we are. To accomplish this, we increase our ability to discern the Lord's direction and counsel by developing a consistent, intimate, morning prayer routine.

———————

Pray the morning offering.

———————

Meditate on the daily Gospel—the 7 R's of prayer.

———————

Pray a Scriptural Rosary decade(s).

———————

Practice 15 minutes of prayer / 5 minutes silence

(using *The Liturgy of Hours* or Sacred Scripture as a basis of prayer).

Day 5

(Lent Week 1: Sunday)

INVOCATION: JESUS, HELP ME TO RESPOND TO
YOUR CALL TO FOLLOW YOU.

THE SACRED SUMMONS

Jesus Calls His Disciples

———

"Come ye after me." Matthew 4:19

Innate to human experience is the nearly automated desire to be respected, wanted, and selected. To be esteemed and chosen by those who are most esteemed is a rare and cherished accomplishment. One cannot choose to be elite, but rather the elite must choose him. Men are all too familiar with the acute pain and discouragement associated with being rejected instead of being selected.

During Jesus' life on earth, the most regarded and essential element of Judaism was the Torah and the interpretation of the Law. At the age of five, a male Jew attended his local synagogue for the purpose of learning Hebrew and memorizing the Torah. By the age of thirteen (*bar mitzvah*), a typical male Jew would have memorized the Torah (also called the Pentateuch, meaning the first five books of the Old Testament), the *Nevium* (the prophets), and the *Kituvin* (the writings), which comprised all of the Hebrew Scripture.

The young men who demonstrated great skill in their studies were selected to learn from the sages how to interpret the Torah (also known as "the Yoke of the Torah"). If, by the age of seventeen, the boy had advanced, he would enter *yeshiva*, learning how to interpret God's Word as it relates to the practical issues of daily living.

After identifying a young man who had ascended the ranks of rabbinic training and had the potential to become like his rabbi, his rabbi would say to him, "Follow me; take my yoke upon you" (the yoke being the rabbi's interpretation of the Torah).

Only those of supreme intelligence, persistence, and potential to interpret God's Word were selected. Because of this, eventually, the realm of religion, the fulfillment of religious precepts, and the pursuit of righteousness were understood as being the exclusive sphere of the intellectually elite.

Consequently, often the Jewish religious leaders became puffed up with pride, laying heavy spiritual burdens on the people by multiplying the legal demands and religious prescriptions of the Law.

So infected were the teachers of the Law with the plague of pride that, after receiving testimony from the man born blind who was healed by Jesus, they retorted, "Thou wast wholly born in sins, and dost thou teach us? And they cast him out" (Jn 9:34). The Pharisees' behavior demonstrates that though one appears devoted and religious, if he is puffed up with pride, he, without perceiving it, is blind to the truth.

Indeed, our Lord warned His disciples and is warning us, "Take heed and beware of the leaven of the Pharisees and Sadducees" (Mt

16:6). Leaven was understood by the first-century Jew as a symbol of sin. As leaven puffs up, so also does pride, and pride is the most heinous of sins. As St. Paul counseled, "'Knowledge puffeth up; but charity edifieth" (1 Cor 8:1).

Here, again, we encounter the irony of the mind of Christ. At the onset of Jesus' public ministry, after His victory over temptation in the wilderness, the itinerant rabbi begins to choose those who will constitute His inner circle of disciples. However, unlike the rabbis of His day, Jesus did not summon the qualified but rather qualified those whom He summoned. Jesus did not look abroad, nor recruit those with the finest pedigree, intellect, or gifts, but gathered local, ordinary, uneducated men for His disciples.

Among the members of Christ's chosen band was a man who would eventually attempt to decapitate another man—Malchus, the high priest's slave—but instead severed his ear from his head. Yet, Christ selected Peter as chief of the Apostles and vicar of His emerging Church.

Also among His chosen twelve was a man who extorted money from his fellow Jews. Yet, Christ called Matthew, the most egregious kind of tax collector, to be so intimate with Him that the disciple became a key witness of Jesus' life and penned one of the Gospels of Christ.

In addition to His chosen twelve, Jesus appointed a man who committed human genocide by slaughtering and imprisoning members of the nascent Church. Yet, Paul, "who persecuted [Christians] in times past," began to "preach the faith which once he impugned" (Gal 1:23).

It is most evident that Jesus is not interested in calling the gifted but rather with gifting those that He calls. Christ receives the lowly and exalts them (see Lk 1:52) that the glory of God may be manifest in weakness (see 2 Cor 12:9).

Indeed, to follow a first-century rabbi was a heavy yoke. The world and, at times, religious leaders continue to burden men with the yoke of "measuring up." The underlying message is that God is not for the little ones, the uneducated, the common folk, or the sinner, but for the spiritual elite. In other words, one must make a name for himself and demonstrate his worth that he may be esteemed as spiritually elite.

Yet, Christ calls you to "take up [his] yoke upon you, and learn of [him], because [he is] meek, and humble of heart: and you shall find rest to your souls" (Mt 11:29).

Jesus commands us to learn from Him and find rest in the truth that the essence of religion is not confined to rules but rather a relationship with Him. Indeed, rules are at the service of a relationship, rather than a relationship being defined by rules. Even the most renowned of rabbis, even with his knowledge of the Law, cannot justify himself before God; yet, we may be justified by God by knowing the greatest rabbi.

If you, my son, desire to be a great leader, it is imperative that you learn to follow. If you desire to lead others to Christ, you must humble yourself to led by Christ. Yet, Jesus does not summon the proud who believe themselves capable of carrying heavy yokes but rather the spiritually weak through whom His power can be manifest. Christ invites you, "Come, follow me" (Mk 10:21), but, to do so, you must cast off the yoke of pride, for, if you exalt yourself, God has no need for you. Yet, if you admit your need for God, in due time, He will exalt you.

Lord Jesus, burn the image of your holy face into me
that I may become a revelation of your glory,
that I may proclaim as did the holy Apostle:
"It is no longer I who live, but Christ who lives in me." Amen.

———

Optional Scripture Readings: Mark 1:16–20;

Matthew 4:17–20; Matthew 11:19–30

———

FULFILL YOUR SELECTED SPIRITUAL PRACTICES FROM STAGE 2:
CALLING AND CLEANSING.

Day 6

(Lent Week 1: Monday)

INVOCATION: JESUS, HELP ME TO DISCERN YOUR VOICE,
AND LISTEN TO YOUR WORD.

THE FOUNDATION OF THE SPIRITUAL LIFE

Jesus Teaches His Disciples the Spiritual Life's
First Essential: Listening to the Word

"Not in bread alone doth man live." Matthew 4:4

In the modern age, even amongst Christians, warped misconceptions of man's relationship to and with God have emerged. Often man misinterprets the purpose of the spiritual life as being at the service of his temporal welfare, the supernatural as a means to nurture the natural, or God's existence for the purpose of blessing and prolonging man's temporal life.

Rather than using the temporal as a means to build the spiritual life, man often erroneously thinks that God exists to serve his flesh. St. Paul described this misguided approach as seeking the things that are below rather than those that are above (see Col 3).

Consider the vast number of Christian men who eat at least three times daily yet rarely allocate time that is dedicated exclusively to God for prayer. The concerns for the flesh slow the eagerness of the spirit, while the enlivened soul subdues the flesh and uses it for spiritual progress.

Responding to Satan's temptation to turn stone into bread, the famished Jesus replied, "Not in bread alone doth man live, but by every word that proceedeth from the mouth of God" (Mt 4:4). Once again, Jesus confronts our misguided approach to life and our common misconceptions of God. Though the body is good and a gift from God, and must be nurtured, the soul has priority over the body. The soul "refers to the innermost aspect of man, that which is of greatest value in him, that by which he most especially is in God's image: 'soul' signifies the *spiritual principle* in man" (CCC 363). The "soul is the form of the body."[5]

As the body depends upon sustenance to survive, so also the soul, which is the greatest value in man, is nurtured by the Word of God. God entrusts very few with His Word because there are few that hunger for the Word of God. More concerned are men with feeding their bellies than nurturing their souls, and, therefore, their souls and bodies both suffer. All too often, the exterior behavior and habits of our flesh deform and damage our interior life. To be conquerors of the flesh, it is imperative to know that the interior life gives the exterior life form and build one's spiritual life on that principle.

The defect in this matter is not with God but with man. The Word always speaks but rarely finds one willing to listen. There exist many who proclaim God's Word yet are inattentive to His

5   St. Thomas Aquinas, *Shorter Summa*, 297.

voice. There are many men who act in the name and power of God's authority yet neglect to submit to the authority and power of God by attentively discerning God's divine counsel.

God clearly communicates His desire of man: "Sacrifice and offering thou dost not desire; but thou hast given me an open ear" (Ps 40:6; RSV). Indeed, "Blessed are they who hear the word of God, and keep it" (Lk 11:28). God seeks men who listen.

To obey God, one must listen and discern His divine counsel. Obedience presupposes that one has listened, so listening is the beginning of obedience. Furthermore, "Obedience is better than sacrifices: and to hearken rather than to offer the fat of rams" (1 Sm 15:22). God is not as interested in your deeds as much as in your attentiveness to His divine directives. For by discerning His counsel, you become more capable of doing those works that He actually desires. As St. John of the Cross tells us:

> Let those, then, who are singularly active, who think they can win the world with their preaching and exterior works, observe here that they would profit the Church and please God much more, not to mention the good example they would give, were they to spend at least half of this time with God in prayer. . . . They would then certainly accomplish more, and with less labor, by one work than they otherwise would by a thousand. For through their prayer they would merit this result, and themselves be spiritually strengthened. Without prayer they would do a great deal of hammering but accomplish little, and sometimes nothing, and even at times cause harm.[6]

---

6   St. John of the Cross, *Spiritual Canticle*, 29, 3.

Recall how Martha, frustrated with her sister Mary for sitting and listening to Jesus and not assisting her in serving the Lord and His disciples, chided Jesus, imploring Him to command Mary to rise and help her serve. To which Jesus responded, "One thing is necessary. Mary hath chosen the best part, which shall not be taken away from her" (Lk 10:42).

As the soul has priority over the body, so also listening has priority over and precedes doing. Indeed, listening to Jesus' word is the "best part," which consequently leads to obedient action.

My son, if you aspire to be God's voice, it is imperative to be attentive to His Word. If you believe truly that your soul has priority over your body, give prayer the pride of place. Build your day around God, rather than God around your day.

"Seek the things that are above; where Christ is sitting at the right hand of God" (Col 3:1), which is the Word that proceeds from God, "not the things that are upon the earth" (Col 3:2), which is bread alone. To seek the things of the earth first, is to place God last.

Therefore, my son, "seek ye therefore first the kingdom of God, and his justice, and all these things shall be added unto you" (Mt 6:33).

Lord Jesus, burn the image of your holy face into me
that I may become a revelation of your glory,
that I may proclaim as did the holy Apostle:
"It is no longer I who live, but Christ who lives in me." Amen.

Optional Scripture Readings: Luke 10:38–42; Colossians 3:1–5

FULFILL YOUR SELECTED SPIRITUAL PRACTICES FROM STAGE 2:
CALLING AND CLEANSING.

Day 7

(Lent Week 1: Tuesday)

INVOCATION: JESUS, GIVE ME THE GRACE TO BE OBEDIENT TO YOUR WORD.

THE WORKS OF THE SPIRITUAL LIFE

*Jesus Teaches His Disciples the Spiritual Life's
Second Essential: Obedience to the Word*

"Do whatever he tells you." John 2:5, RSV

Burdened by human expectations, man is often conditioned, if not compelled, to measure himself by worldly standards. One must be conspicuous rather than overlooked and considered great rather than common. He ought to have more that he may not be regarded as less. He is to appear strong by masking his weakness. He should attempt to build a life of comfort by avoiding suffering and pursue freedom by casting off submission to a greater authority.

The core and center of the spirit of the world is a motivation for personal success, self-gratification, and worldly glory, often obtained at the expense of others. Yet, Christ's ways are not the world's ways. The Son of God became flesh to reveal His Father and the manner by which His Father works, that we may know how to participate in His work and become partakers in His glory.

Both God and the devil propose glory, and, therefore, it is imperative that we discern the difference between the two that we may discern the counterfeit from the divine reality.

The setting for the inauguration of Jesus' public ministry occurred at "a marriage in Cana of Galilee: and the mother of Jesus was there. And Jesus also was invited, and his disciples, to the marriage" (Jn 2:1–2).

The duration of a typical Jewish wedding was seven days, giving ample time for relatives and friends, often who traveled long distances to attend the celebratory feast. On this occasion, however, in the midst of the celebration, the wine ran out. To be depleted of wine during a marriage feast was a social catastrophe. Mary, Jesus' Mother, alerted her Son of the dilemma: "They have no wine" (Jn 2:3).

To which Jesus responded, "Woman, what is that to me and to thee? my hour is not yet come" (Jn 2:4).

Mary turned to the waiters, saying, "Whatsoever he shall say to you, do ye" (Jn 2:5).

Jesus then commanded the servants to fill six stone jars—each capable of holding twenty to thirty gallons—with water (see Jn 2:6–7).

Here, we ought to pause and reflect. Why, when the newly married couple desperately needed wine, did Jesus command the servants to gather water? Certainly, the servants interpreted the Lord's command as illogical and incapable of fulfilling the present need. Nevertheless, the servants obediently filled the jars "to the brim" (Jn 2:7).

Jesus then transformed the water the servants had gathered into wine, and not just any common wine, but the best wine, as testified to by the chief steward of the feast who said to the bridegroom, "Every man at first setteth forth good wine, and when men have well drunk, then that which is worse. But thou hast kept the good wine until now" (Jn 2:10).

The water that the servants gathered is a symbol of man's works, his meager efforts, which in the end cannot sufficiently provide a divine remedy. Indeed, man cannot accomplish anything without Christ (see Jn 15:5). Christ, however, desires our works, our efforts, our water, that He may have something with which He can transform into wine, which is a rich symbol of grace.

Jesus wills that the Christian man respond with faith to His commands by doing those works that can only be identified as the apparently insignificant, the common, the ordinary, and, at times, the illogical.

Christ requests of us works that are animated by the motive to remain hidden and humble rather than to be noticed—works of charity that are characterized by silence rather than being loud and proud. He desires us to give to others when we are the ones in need, to embrace sacrifice for others rather than comfort ourselves, to be humble rather than self-exalted, to love our weaknesses rather than to relish our own strength, and to submit obediently to our enemies rather than to seek retaliation.

To "do whatever He tells you" demands that the servant of Jesus has great faith in the miraculous power of God, who transforms the natural into the supernatural, the insignificant into that which is significant, and man's littleness and weakness into His greatness and strength.

This battle to believe that God can do much with our little will be a perennial testing ground for the Christian man. The devil will continually and relentlessly barrage him with the sense that his life of common banality is of little difference to God or to His kingdom, particularly as he succumbs to comparing himself to worldly achievers.

It is Christ who will transform your common water, your hidden sacrificial works of obedience, into grace for yourself and others, if the character of your works are hidden and humble.

To have the mind of Christ is to be faithful in small matters (see Lk 16:10). Or, more precisely: "He that is faithful in that which is least, is faithful also in that which is greater" (Lk 16:10). Indeed, the Lord will make him ruler over many things (see Mt 25:21).

My son, without Christ, your water—your charitable works—regardless of their perceived honorary value, can never become wine. Nor without your water will Christ make wine. The tender paradox of an all-powerful God is that He wills that a mutual participation occurs between the Creator and the creature, between the Father and the son, and that a collaboration transpires between Him, who can accomplish all without us, and us, who can accomplish nothing without Him.

Jesus's first public miracle occurring in the context of a wedding feast is an unmistakable sign that God wills a marriage a mutual participation—of works between the divine and human, between God and man.

Again, the Son of God became flesh to reveal His Father and the manner by which His Father works—humbly and in hiddenness—that we may know how to participate in His work and become partakers in His glory.

Lord Jesus, burn the image of your holy face into me
that I may become a revelation of your glory,
that I may proclaim as did the holy Apostle:
"It is no longer I who live, but Christ who lives in me." Amen.

Optional Scripture Readings John 2:1–11; Luke 16:1–15

FULFILL YOUR SELECTED SPIRITUAL PRACTICES FROM STAGE 2:
CALLING AND CLEANSING.

Day 8

(Lent Week 1: Wednesday)

INVOCATION: JESUS, GIVE ME THE GRACE TO
TAKE UP MY CROSS DAILY.

THE SACRED DEMANDS

Jesus Teaches the Disciples the Spiritual Life's
Third Essential: Embracing the Cross

———

"Let him deny himself, and take up his cross,
and follow me." Matthew 16:24

To live for oneself perhaps is the easiest thing a man can do. Selfishness, the path of least resistance, is the wide gate, the broad way that many traverse only for it to terminate in their own perdition. Whereas self-denial is the arduous narrow gate, the less traveled rocky path, that leads to eternal glory and true, perpetual, unfailing happiness.

Self-denial, however, for its own sake is a kind of self-mastery, which in itself can become laden with and disfigured by self-preoccupation. Self-denial that is characterized by surrendering or sacrificing something for the sake of another's well-being is meritorious and life-giving.

We have received from our most Blessed Mother the command to do whatever He tells us (see Jn 2:5), and so now we turn to Christ to discover His sacred demands upon the man who desires to follow Him in earnest.

Speaking to the crowds who had become fascinated with Him, His message, and His miracles, Christ shatters any false notions of a Christian being an effeminate follower: "If any man will come after me, let him deny himself, and take up his cross, and follow me" (Mt 16:24). This threefold divine command is the foundation of the Christian man's work and walk with Christ, for, if he neglects or rejects to carry his own cross and follow after Jesus, he cannot be His disciple.

To the Jew, who understood the cross as a Roman form of torture and execution, Jesus' words must have been incomprehensible. As we follow Christ, a consistent theme emerges: Christ's perspective and His very approach to a fulfilled life, to obtaining happiness, and to receiving salvation and the plenitude of divine beatitude runs contrary to the world's proposal that happiness can be obtained by satiating one's passions. To the world, denying oneself appears to be a harsh personal deprivation that robs a man of joy, consolation, and personal freedom.

Jesus knows that man, in the depth of his soul, desires authentic freedom. But man often misunderstands the meaning of freedom and, without the aid of grace and divine prudence, is incapable of comprehending or achieving it. Man interprets freedom as personal license, the exercise of autonomy unhindered by authority or its hierarchical constraints, and, therefore, seeks to bend to the desires of the flesh, while systematically ignoring the moral and eternal consequences of such slavery to the senses.

This type of freedom is precisely the slavery that binds man in the discouraging, if not maddening, sadness of not being satiated by creatures. In fact, it is impossible that a lesser creature can fulfill a greater creature who is created for the Creator.[7]

Desiring to liberate us from slavery to our passions and provide the grace for us to live in the freedom of sons of God, Jesus gives us the paradoxical command to deny ourselves. Associated with the idea of self-denial is a misconceived morbid sense of sadness, a cold and rigid soul void of all joy and consolation. The paradox of self-denial is that in giving oneself away one always receives. By denying oneself of personal attachments for the sake of the other, a man carves out a spiritual space in his soul for God to dwell—and with God comes the plentitude of peace, joy, and unsurpassed charity.

It is a great irony that the more a man possesses the more he is possessed by the fear of losing what he has. Yet, when a man gives what he owns, he conquers the fear of having less, for he experiences the Lord's continual provision. Indeed, as the Lord Jesus says, "He that shall lose his life for me, shall find it" (Mt 10:39), and "It is a more blessed thing to give, rather than to receive" (Acts 20:35).

Second, Jesus summons us to take up our cross and embrace it as our own. The cross has, in our modern age, become an icon of beauty or a symbol used as a way to identify oneself as a Christian. Jesus' Cross, however, was synonymous with His execution, His shame before men, His physical powerlessness, and His death. Christ's Cross represented His loss of human freedom, dignity, and honor. The Cross is a striking and shocking spectacle of tortured

7   See St. Catherine of Siena, *Dialogue*, Suzanne Noffke, O.P., Paulist Press, 19080, Section 48, p 98.

bodily nakedness that speaks of complete vulnerability and defenselessness. By taking up His Cross, "him, who knew no sin, he hath made sin for us" (2 Cor 5:21) and "bore our sins in his body upon the tree" (1 Pt 2:24). The Cross, then, is the definitive symbol of God's love for man. God on the Cross is totally self-giving and completely vulnerable. Jesus on the Cross is the fully lived expression of self-donation for the sake of the other. Jesus willed to drink deeply from the dregs of death for the purpose that man, who is so easily overcome with doubt and distrust, would be certain that God is not against him but rather for him (see Rom 8:31).

The tremendous irony of the Cross is that those who endure its pains appear to be momentarily alone, yet will be surrounded by love. But Jesus assures us, "Unless a grain of wheat falls to the ground and dies, it remains alone" (Jn 12:24, RSV). Those who refrain from bearing their cross for the sake of the other, for the sake of souls, in the end, are alone and isolated. Why? Love begets love. One who loves receives love. One who resists loving will resist being loved. Indeed, Jesus speaks to this truth when He says, "And I, if I be lifted up from the earth, will draw all things to myself" (Jn 12:32).

Human beings are instinctively and magnetically attracted to those who sacrifice and are sacrificed for the sake of others. We intuitively respect and admire those who, for the sake of their fellow man, have shed their blood. Yet, within man is a visceral abhorrence for those who slothfully and selfishly flee from aiding their neighbor in need. Self-donation, symbolized by the Cross, is the magnet that draws people to rich communion with, and empathy and compassion for, their fellow man.

Once again, the mind of Christ, in whom is the fullness of wisdom (see Col 2:3), proposes a way to unfailing happiness that runs in complete opposition to the world's methods of attaining it: self-donation. Indeed, "the word of the cross is folly to those who are perishing, but to us who are being saved it is the power of God" (1 Cor 1:18, RSV).

My son, if you seek power—the power to overcome vice, fallen passions, and even your self-preoccupation—you will only discover such freedom by taking up your cross and following Christ.

Lord Jesus, burn the image of your holy face into me
that I may become a revelation of your glory,
that I may proclaim as did the holy Apostle:
"It is no longer I who live, but Christ who lives in me." Amen.

Optional Scripture Readings: John 12:24–32; Matthew 16:24–27

FULFILL YOUR SELECTED SPIRITUAL PRACTICES FROM STAGE 2:
CALLING AND CLEANSING.

Day 9

(Lent Week 1: Thursday)

INVOCATION: JESUS, GIVE ME THE GRACE TO
ONLY DESIRE TO GLORIFY YOU.

SECRET SERVICE

Jesus Teaches His Disciples the Spiritual Life's
Fourth Essential: Overcoming the Trap of Vainglory

———

"Pray to thy Father in secret." Matthew 6:6

B oasting, posturing, and seeking recognition, though disor-dered behaviors, are indicators that a man has been created and destined for glory. For at the foundation of these false desires is the true, authentic desire for divine glory. Yet, these behaviors also imply man's lack of confidence and certainty that God will glorify him, and, therefore, man succumbs to attempting to glorify himself.

It is not a sin to acknowledge or approve our own goodness. Rather, God requires it of us.[8] To reject ones' own goodness is

———

8   See St. Thomas Aquinas, *Summa Theologiae*, Book 2, Article 1.

to reject the God who created man to be good. Glory becomes perverted when we attempt to usurp the glory that belongs to God and claim it for ourselves. This is, in fact, a form of robbery.

Threaded throughout the Gospels is the reoccurring theme of the Pharisees who love the seats of honor in the synagogues (see Lk 11:43; Mt 23:6), who pray in the marketplaces to be seen by others (see Mt 6:5), who widen their phylacteries and lengthen their tassels for exterior show (see Mt 23:5), and who perform all their works to be seen by men (see Mt 23:5).

The Pharisee is the human embodiment of the insecure, unconfident man who is enslaved to human opinion. He maliciously uses religion and religious prescriptions to his advantage for the purpose of measuring his external performance and, consequently, as a means to judge others' sanctity, or lack thereof.

Ultimately, the purpose of the self-righteous Pharisee is to be the victor in the arena of comparison. Externally, he exudes piety and righteousness, while, internally, he is vexed by jealousy, envy, resentment, and bitterness, particularly at the sight of his brother's progression in holiness or gaining of respect from fellow men. The goodness of glory becomes twisted into the sin of vainglory when our desire for earthly prestige, human praise, and temporal honors replaces our desire to glorify God.

"Why do you love vanity?" God asks (see Ps 4:3) for "even the love of praise is sinful."[9] "Vainglory enters secretly, and robs us insensibly, of all our inward possessions,"[10] and, therefore, we must "be aware of the desire for glory since it enslaves the mind."[11]

---

9   St. Augustine, St. Thomas Aquinas, *Summa Theologiae*, Book 2, Article 1.
10   St. John Chrysostom, *ibid.*
11   St. Thomas Aquinas, *ibid.*

Our Lord Jesus understands man's pathetic condition and is sympathetic to his plight. Jesus knows that the man who does not see, feel, or hear God's approval is gravely tempted and lured into seeking vainglory. Too often, man surrenders his desire for the consolation of heaven in exchange for his pride to be consoled by men. For this reason, Christ commands us to pray in secret, fast in secret, and give alms in secret so that our Father, who also sees in secret, will repay us (see Mt 6:6).

The divine physician gives man the antidote to the illness of vainglory by summoning us to the life of Christian secrecy. His remedy is counterintuitive to the ways of men. Indeed, to partake in divine glory by remaining unnoticed and hidden (secret) appears to be illogical. Man, often afraid of being forgotten, unimportant, and unneeded, rejects Christ's invitation to the secret life. But, to those who accept His invitation, He promises that "there is not any thing secret that shall not be made manifest, nor hidden, that shall not be known and come abroad" (Lk 8:17).

A life of habitual secrecy gradually grinds away the enslaving habit of seeking the consolation and admiration of men. Eventually, freedom from human opinion is acquired, and God's peace enters the man, enabling him to be at peace with himself and with God.

The Christian attribute of secrecy is often misunderstood as a consequence rather than an intention. It is erroneous to attempt to control the outcome of our actions—whether we are noticed and praised by men, or not. God only asks us to be responsible for our motivations, ensuring that the spirit animating our actions is one of secrecy, while trusting that God ultimately determines the outcome.

The life of Christ is marked by the character of secrecy: He was conceived without a human father or his knowledge of His conception, born in a desolate manger, and spent His childhood in an obscure village, all while His supernatural powers remained cloaked and veiled. So common was Christ that the Nazarene villagers were scandalized by Him, saying, "Is not this the carpenter's son?" (Mt 13:55). Those who knew Jesus were aware that He was not educated and that He did not receive formal training from any of the renowned rabbis.

Repeatedly, after healing an individual, Jesus commanded the recipient of the miracle to "tell no one" (Mk 7:36, RSV) what He had done for them. When Jesus understood, after performing the miracle of the loaves and the fishes, that the people intended to make Him King of Israel by force, He fled to the mountains to hide in solitude (see Jn 6:15). Furthermore, the most glorious, life-altering, pivotal event in the history of humanity—Christ's Resurrection from the dead—was accomplished privately, in the dark, early hours of the Easter morning watch.

Nevertheless, Jesus' life, which was hidden, has been revealed. Christ "let [his] light shine before men, that they may . . . glorify [his] Father who is in heaven" (Mt 5:16). Christ did not force others to notice His light—He simply shined. Truth is like light. Light enters darkness, and darkness flees from the light. The truth of Christ casts out darkness.

Glory, according to St. Augustine, is clarity—someone's good that is clearly seen. If you become like Christ, you will have no need to obtain attention from creatures, for your very life will run so contrary to the world that you cannot help but be conspicuous.

To be unconquerable in Christ is to be liberated from the bondage to vainglory and human recognition. My son, pray, give, and fast to your Father *who is in secret*, and seeing you in secret, your heavenly Father will reward you (see Mt 6:6).

+ JMJ +

Lord Jesus, burn the image of your holy face into me
that I may become a revelation of your glory,
that I may proclaim as did the holy Apostle:
"It is no longer I who live, but Christ who lives in me." Amen.

———

Optional Scripture Readings: Matthew 5:14–16; Matthew 6:1–6

———

FULFILL YOUR SELECTED SPIRITUAL PRACTICES FROM STAGE 2:
CALLING AND CLEANSING.

Day 10

(Lent Week 1: Friday)

INVOCATION: JESUS, CLEANSE MY TEMPLE OF ALL FALSE IDOLS.

PURGING THE TEMPLE OF GOD

Jesus Cleanses the Temple

"Blessed is he that cometh in the name of the Lord" Matthew 21:9

Directly preceding the culminating moment of every Holy Sacrifice of the Mass, the moment when the substances of the bread and wine are transubstantiated into the Body and Blood of Jesus Christ, the faithful assembly falls to their knees after chanting *"Sanctus, Sanctus, Sanctus, Dóminus Deus Sabaóth..."* (Holy, Holy, Holy Lord God of hosts.... Blessed is he who comes in the name of the Lord. Hosanna in the highest.).[12]

These words of the Mass echo and commemorate the occasion of Jesus' triumphal entry into Jerusalem. As He entered the city, riding an ass, "a very great multitude spread their garments in the way: and others cut boughs from the trees, and strewed them in the

12 *Roman Missal*, 83.

way: And the multitudes that went before and that followed, cried, saying: Hosanna to the son of David: Blessed is he that cometh in the name of the Lord: Hosanna in the highest" (Mt 21:8–9).

The celebratory throng and praises of the people were suddenly interrupted by an event, which from a religious, political, diplomatic perspective was utterly devastating. Unexpectedly, with the rapidity and surge of a lighting striking, Jesus' anger was enkindled. With indignant rage, Christ's just wrath was vented upon those traders who occupied His Father's Temple, converting it into a marketplace rather than a holy place of worship.

"And when he had made, as it were, a scourge of little cords, he drove them all out of the temple, the sheep also and the oxen, and the money changers he poured out, and the tables he overthrew" (Jn 2:15), saying, "My house shall be called the house of prayer; but you have made it a den of thieves" (Mt 21:13).

To appreciate sufficiently our Lord's just indignation, it is necessary that we comprehend the context of His cleansing of the Temple in Jerusalem. At that time:

Every Jew has to pay a temple tax of one half-shekel a year. That was equivalent to nearly two day's wages for a working man . . . It was paid at the Passover time. Jews came from all over the world to the Passover with all kinds of currencies. When they went to have their money changed, they had to pay a fee, and should their coin exceed the tax, they had to pay another fee before they got their change . . . and the commission amounted to a half a day's wage, which for most people was a great deal of money.[13]

13   William Barclay, *Gospel of Mark*, Louisville, Kentucky, Westminster Knox Press, 1975, 318.

Additionally, pilgrims were required by the Law to bring sacrificial victims without blemish and offer them to the Lord. However, Temple inspectors often rejected the pilgrims' offerings and demanded that they purchase the doves and lambs at the Temple stables. "The price of a pair of doves inside [the Temple] could be as much fifteen times the price that might be paid outside."[14]

The Temple marketplace was known as Annas's Bazaar. Annas was the father-in-law of Caiaphas, who reigned as high priest of the Jews from 6–15 AD and had authority and charge over the Temple's finances, administration, and collection of taxes. Though Annas's term as high priest ended in 15 AD, he virtually reigned, monopolizing the Jewish priesthood through four successors, three of which were his own sons. His fourth successor, his son-in-law, Joseph Caiaphas, was the man who condemned Jesus to death.

Jesus' cleansing of the Temple and reclaiming it as a "house of prayer" was certainly interpreted by Annas and the priestly class as a crushing condemnation of their usurpation of the Temple and their relentless extortion of money from God's people. Christ's zeal for His Father and His Father's house (see Jn 2:17; Ps 69:9), and His passionate desire to liberate souls that they may truly worship, made Jesus a real threat to the priestly class.

The Temple in Jerusalem functioned as the center of Jewish worship where the faithful thought heaven and earth could unite, affording those who were present an encounter with the living God. Indeed, part and parcel to the faith of the Jews was the belief that the Temple in Jerusalem was the footstool of God's presence, the *Biet HaMickdash*, the "sanctified house." Yet, this holy house had

14 Ibid.

become a marketplace, a den of thieves, and a source of incredible revenue for the dynasty of Annas.

By means of the sacrament of Baptism, God has made you into His holy dwelling, a *Biet HaMickdash*. Yet, "do you not know that you are God's temple?" (1 Cor 3:16, RSV). How often does man grieve the Holy Spirit who dwells in him (see Eph 4:30) by making the Father's temple, which he is, into a den of thieves.

Be aware, my son, that God does not love us in halves but desires our entirety. He wants possession of you that you may possess Him. He wills to abide in you that you may abide in Him, and He wants all of you that you may be all in Him, so "that God may be all in all" (1 Cor 15:28). Indeed, God desires to dwell in your temple that you may be holy, but, to dwell therein, your temple needs cleansing.

Created things are a sign of the Creator's goodness and benevolence toward man. Sin is never a reality in itself but rather is always attached to some kind of good, thereby maligning its good nature. For this reason, sin becomes appealing in that it is concealed in and attached to something good and desirable.

God understands that man desires the good and yet is often seduced by a good tainted by sin. One of the devil's strategies is to dupe man into desiring the good more than that which is great, into loving the creature over and above the Creator, and into becoming attached to the gift rather than allowing the gift to lead man to the Giver of all good gifts. When a man submits to this, the temple of God, which he is, becomes a temple of thieves.

The soul of man often experiences a kind of perpetual torture, as his temple toggles between belonging to God or to the devil. Indeed, if you have embarked upon the arduous yet rewarding quest to follow and become another Christ, your heart will not allow or endure being divided. As our Lord says, "No man can serve two masters. For either he will hate the one, and love the other: or he will sustain the one, and despise the other. You cannot serve God and mammon" (Mt 6:24).

As you attend the Holy Sacrifice of the Mass and pray, "Blessed is he who comes in the name of the Lord," remember that "THY KING will come to thee, the just and saviour" (Zec 9:9) as holy food. If you, my son, are not attentive to cleansing your temple, Christ will do it for you—for He loves you and desires that you experience His love. Make it your aim to begin to separate yourself from those things that separate you from Christ, lest, in His holy desire to save you, you undergo the day of His purging.

Lord Jesus, burn the image of your holy face into me
that I may become a revelation of your glory,
that I may proclaim as did the holy Apostle,
"It is no longer I who live, but Christ who lives in me." Amen.

———————

Optional Scripture Readings: Matthew 21:7–16; John 2:13–22

———————

FULFILL YOUR SELECTED SPIRITUAL PRACTICES FROM STAGE 2:
CALLING AND CLEANSING.

+ JMJ +

Day 11

(Lent Week 1: Saturday)

INVOCATION: JESUS, GIVE ME THE GRACE TO RECEIVE YOUR MERCY
AND, BY RECEIVING MERCY, BECOME CAPABLE OF GIVING IT.

THE ESSENTIAL CHRISTIAN CHARACTER

Jesus Is Tested by the Pharisees

"Neither will I condemn thee." John 8:11

Cheap mercy is a modern phenomenon wherein man does not
comprehend the cost of the forgiveness that he has received, for
he does not comprehend the tremendous depth of his sinful debt.
Modern man minimizes his sins as inconsequential misgivings,
believing that he is undeserving of damnation, for he evaluates himself
to be "a good man" or, at the very least, not an evil man, and, therefore, he deems mercy as an unneeded, superficial, spiritual formality.

The word mercy is derived from the Latin word *merces*, which
means to "pay the price." To be merciful is to forgive, and the act of
forgiveness demands that one relieve another of his debt owed. And
this debt has an associated cost for the one who has been victim-
ized. To forgive is to pay the price of another's sins.

Responding to St. Peter's question, "Lord, how often shall my brother offend against me, and I forgive him? till seven times? (Mt 18:21), Jesus told the parable of the unforgiving steward (see Mt 18:23–35).

Jesus tells of a steward who, being responsible for his master's estate, is summoned by the master to settle accounts. The steward has accrued a massive debt equal to 10,000 talents. A talent was a weight used to measure Greek and Roman coins. A talent was worth 6,000 denarii, and a denarius was the equivalent of a Roman soldier's daily wage. The value of a talent then was approximately nineteen years' wages, which indicates that this man owed his master 190,000 years of wages. The steward's debt amounted to nearly 2,500 lifetimes of work.

How difficult it is to comprehend the magnitude of debt the steward amassed. If a man were to work his entire life and offer every penny to his master, he would have only paid .0004% of the debt mentioned above.

"But that servant falling down, besought him, saying: Have patience with me, and I will pay thee all. And the lord of that servant being moved with pity, let him go and forgave him the debt" (Mt 18:26–27).

With this parable, Christ discloses the two-fold reality of the unfathomable cost of our sins and God's limitless ability to forgive our debt. In truth, our sins constitute a debt that we are incapable of ever restoring, regardless of how many lifetimes we could dedicate to Christ's service. For this reason, the psalmist says, "No brother can redeem, nor shall man redeem: he shall not give to God his ransom" (Ps 49:7–8). "Therefore no one will be declared righteous in God's sight by the works of the law" (Rom 3:20, NIV). No merit of his own, therefore, can justify a man in the sight of God. "The

Lawgiver was not unaware that the burden of the law exceeded the power of men. But he judged this useful so men might become aware of their own insufficiency. Therefore in commanding impossible things, God has made men humble. Because truly, none of us will ever by justified in God's sight by works of the law."[15]

Man, blinded by sin, often is oblivious that he has infected his fellow man with his sin and, therefore, does not comprehend his immense need for mercy. Indeed, 2,500 lifetimes of work is a symbol of the number of souls a human infects with his sins during his brief life. Conviction is a necessary requirement for our conversion to Christ. We must feel, as did the steward in Christ's parable, the pain and horror of our guilt. Typically, this pain becomes comprehensible when a man receives a just sentence for his transgressions. The just sentence awakens him from his stupor of sinfulness and opens his soul to thirsting for God's mercy.

The Pharisees "bring unto [Jesus] a woman taken in adultery" (Jn 8:3), testing Him by asking if she should be condemned: "Now Moses in the law commanded us to stone such a one. But what sayest thou?" (Jn 8:5). St. John the Evangelist notes, "This they said tempting him, that they might accuse him. But Jesus bowing himself down, wrote with his finger on the ground" (Jn 8:6). Indeed, if Jesus condemns her, He undermines His message of mercy, but, if He releases her from her transgression, He transgresses the Law.

The woman caught in adultery stands condemned. Publicly humiliated, she fears for her life. Only Jesus stood between her and her execution. Yet, this necessary conviction of her sin will serve

---

15 St. Bernard of Clairvaux, *Ralph Martin, The Fulfillment of All Desire,* Steubenville, Ohio, Emmaus Road Publishing.

as her appreciation and gratitude for being forgiven, and Christ's forgiveness will lead to her conversion.

The account of the adulterous woman is rich with profound symbolism. The scribes and Pharisees bring the woman caught in adultery to Jesus. "But Jesus bowing himself down, wrote with his finger in the ground (Jn 8:6). "When therefore they continued asking him, he lifted himself up, and said to them: He that is without sin among you, let him first cast a stone at her" (Jn 8:7). "And again stooping down, he wrote on the ground" (Jn 8:8). After this, the Pharisees, scribes, and ancients left the woman and Jesus alone. "Then Jesus lifting up himself, said to her: Woman, where are they that accused thee? Hath no man condemned thee? . . . Neither will I condemn thee. Go, and now sin no more" (Jn 8:10–11).

Jesus' first act of bowing Himself down and writing with His finger in the earth is a symbol of His Incarnation—His lowering into the dirt from which man was made. The first act of lifting Himself up and issuing the command symbolizes Jesus' life and public teaching in which He raises the exemplary model of mercy. The second occasion that Jesus "stooped down" symbolizes His death and burial into the earth, as if He is writing man's salvation into the dirt of humanity. Thus, His second act of "lifting Himself up" and forgiving the adulterous woman is a profound symbol of Christ's ultimate Resurrection and definitive conquering of sin and death.

Jesus expresses *merces*, that is, He pays the unfathomable price for her sins by means of His death (stooping down) and being lifted up in glory through His Resurrection.

Indeed, you, my son, were condemned in your sin. To receive God's mercy, it is imperative that you acknowledge and receive the just sentence for your sins. Hell was your eternal destined abode.

The devil was to be your master, and infinite was to be your torture. Yet, Christ paid your debt and endured Hell that you may be free of your sin and the consequences thereof.

My son, let us not be like the steward who, after being released from his insurmountable debt, imprisoned his fellow servant who owed him a year of wages. As you have been forgiven by God, so now you must forgive, if you are to continue to receive God's mercy. Therefore, heed the command, "Be ye kind one to another; merciful, forgiving one another, even as God hath forgiven you in Christ" (Eph 4:32). This is the fundamental requirement of the Christian man. He who forgives in Christ because he has been forgiven by Christ remains unconquered in Christ.

Lord Jesus, burn the image of your holy face into me
that I may become a revelation of your glory,
that I may proclaim as did the holy Apostle,
"It is no longer I who live, but Christ who lives in me." Amen.

Optional Scripture Readings: John 8:1–11; Matthew 18:23–35

FULFILL YOUR SELECTED SPIRITUAL PRACTICES FROM STAGE 2:
CALLING AND CLEANSING.

Stage 3

Second Week of Lent
PRECEPTS AND PREPARATION

During this third stage in our Lenten journey, we enter Jesus' divine school, wherein He discloses the spirit that undergirds and animates the Christian's life. Jesus will disclose to us His most precious precepts: charity, sacred responsibility, true hope, true worship, true power, true perfection, and true rest. These foundational precepts of Christ will demand of us a radical shift of mind. Indeed, as we strive to embrace the paradoxical mind of Christ, our Christian worldview and warped worldly approach will be greatly challenged. Yet, this perplexity, if surrendered to God in all humility, will become the catalyst that prompts us to be willing to embrace the ignominious Cross of our Lord Jesus. By means of developing a consistent, attentive evening prayer routine, including an examination of conscience and weekly Confession, we set ourselves to the task of repenting from the world's ways and maxims, and availing ourselves to Christ's precepts.

STAGE 3 SPIRITUAL PRACTICES
(SELECT TWO OR THREE)

The purpose of this stage is to increase our ability to discern the Lord's direction and counsel and identify those habits and sins which are contrary to Christ, that we may repent of them. This is accomplished primarily by frequent examination of conscience and Confession and by developing a consistent and intimate evening prayer.

+ JMJ +

———————

Make an examination of conscience.

———————

Practice 15 minutes of prayer / 5 minutes silence
(using *The Liturgy of Hours* or Sacred Scripture as a basis of prayer).

———————

Pray a Scriptural Rosary decade(s).

———————

Practice spiritual reading.

———————

Go to weekly Confession.

Day 12

(Lent Week 2: Sunday)

INVOCATION: JESUS, GIVE ME THE GRACE TO LOVE MUCH.

REAWAKENING LOVE

Jesus' Precept of Charity

———

"To whom less is forgiven, he loveth less." Luke 7:47

Religious precepts and prescriptions provide a certain and necessary framework to measure and interpret right from wrong. As useful as religious precepts are, they are limited in their power in that the law measures, while love has no measure. Obedience to religious laws must lead to love, lest it becomes a way to justify oneself and to condemn others.

Falling prey to the perennial temptation to reduce religion to a systematic adherence to disciplines and doctrines is ever present in those who lack love for others and lack other's love. The law provides a religious person with a means to judge, rate, evaluate, and assess one's own level of sanctity. Indeed, "the Law was given so that we might seek grace; grace was given so that we might observe the law."[16]

———

16 St. Augustine, *De Spiritu et Littera*, 19, 34.

Only by grace can a man be righteous before God. Therefore, when a man mistakenly uses the law to measure his brother's soul and sanctity, he becomes guilty of transgressing the law. Take heed, "for as many as are of the works of the law, are under a curse. For it is written: Cursed is every one, that abideth not in all things, which are written in the book of the law to do them" (Gal 3:10).

The goodness of the law, religious disciplines, and belief in religious doctrines serve as the perfect gauge by which we can be assured that we stand condemned as sinners. All men sin and have transgressed the commandments of God; therefore, the commandments of God humble us and serve as a compelling reason to seek forgiveness. Yet, it is not the law that compels us to repent, but rather it is the love of Christ that compels us (see 2 Cor 5:14). While the law may condemn a sinner, love alone converts him.

Two of the chief obstacles to the sinner's reception of God's forgiveness are blame and shame. When confronted with our wickedness, we are tempted to blame others, our circumstances, our genealogy, or our physical, emotional, or mental defects rather than accept responsibility for our sinful behavior.

When we blame others, ironically, we are using the law as the basis for our own condemnation. The very law by which we condemn others is the law by which we are condemned. He who measures a man according to the law will be measured by God with the law. "For with what judgment you judge, you shall be judged: and with what measure you mete, it shall be measured to you again" (Mt 7:2).

If a man overcomes the temptation to blame and accepts full responsibility for his sinful behavior, he will inevitably contend with the experience of shame, which is the acute pain, severe humiliation, or distress caused by the consciousness of immoral or foolish behavior. Shame compels man, like Adam, to hide from and avoid God (see Gen 3:8), to cover one's own evil with a false self-justification, and, consequently, to blame others for one's sins.

Perhaps no other account depicts this truth as convincingly as when Jesus dined at the house of Simon the Pharisee. While reclining at table, a woman, who Simon identified as a sinner, threw herself at Jesus' feet, washing them with her tears and wiping them with her hair (see Lk 7:38).

Indignant at the spectacle, Simon "the Pharisee, who had invited him, seeing it, spoke within himself, saying: This man, if he were a prophet, would know surely who and what manner of woman this is that toucheth him, that she is a sinner" (Lk 7:39).

Reading Simon's thoughts, Jesus told a parable: "A certain creditor had two debtors, the one who owed five hundred pence, and the other fifty. And whereas they had not wherewith to pay, he forgave them both. Which therefore of the two loveth him most? Simon answering, said: I suppose that he to whom he forgave the most. And [Jesus] said to him: Thou hast judged rightly" (Lk 7:41–43).

Then Jesus asked Simon a pointed and precise question, "Dost thou see this woman?" (Lk 7:44). By his strict adherence and interpretation of the Law, Simon was conditioned to only measure people by the Law, therefore rendering himself incapable of love. He could not see her goodness beneath her sinful condition.

Simon's lack of love is confirmed by Jesus' recounting of the Pharisee's lack of hospitality towards Christ, "I entered into thy house, thou gavest me no water for my feet; but she with tears hath washed my feet, and with her hairs hath wiped them. Thou gavest me no kiss; but she, since she came in, hath not ceased to kiss my feet. My head with oil thou didst not anoint; but she with ointment hath anointed my feet. Wherefore I say to thee: Many sins are forgiven her, because she hath loved much. But to whom less is forgiven, he loveth less" (Lk 7:44–47).

Christ's words are an echo of His divine judgment in the parable of the Sheep and the Goats: "For I was hungry, and you gave me not to eat: I was thirsty, and you gave me not to drink. I was a stranger, and you took me not in: naked, and you covered me not: sick and in prison, and you did not visit me" (Mt 25:42–43).

My son, if you desire to love much it is necessary to examine your past—but only with God—to understand that you have been forgiven much. To confront one's own wickedness without God, but with the devil, can only lead to despair. God invites you to join Him in confronting your past that you may comprehend the devastating effects that your sins have inflicted upon yourself and others, but always with the knowledge and faith that "God commendeth his charity towards us; because when as yet we were sinners, according to the time, Christ died for us" (Rom 5:8–9).

To paraphrase St. Catherine of Sienna, self-knowledge without knowledge of God will lead to despair, while knowledge of God without self-knowledge leads to presumption. Therefore, knowing our wickedness while having confidence in God's goodness is the means to receiving the love we desire.

The sacrament of Confession is the necessary means and context to receive God's grace and gradually overcome the tendency to blame others; it is the means to overcome shame and take full responsibility for our sins and, thus, receive the fullness of God's forgiveness and mercy in Christ.

When a man sacramentally confesses his sins, he entrusts his vile past to God that God may use it for the purpose of building a hope-filled future in him. Therefore, blame thyself before Christ that thy shame may be removed, for if you be forgiven much in Christ, you will love much in Christ. Indeed, in the end, we will not be judged by the law but by love. Therefore, look upon your brother with love rather than through the law. For "if I should have prophecy and should know all mysteries, and all knowledge, and if I should have all faith, so that I could remove mountains, and have not charity, I am nothing" (1 Cor 13:2).

Lord Jesus, burn the image of your holy face into me
that I may become a revelation of your glory,
that I may proclaim as did the holy Apostle:
"It is no longer I who live, but Christ who lives in me." Amen.

Optional Scripture Readings: Luke 7:36–50; Matthew 7:1–5

FULFILL YOUR SELECTED SPIRITUAL PRACTICES FROM STAGE 3: *PRECEPTS AND PREPARATION.*

Day 13

(Lent Week 2: Monday)

INVOCATION: JESUS, GIVE ME THE GRACE TO BELIEVE THAT
I HAVE BEEN ENTRUSTED WITH MUCH.

REAWAKENING A SENSE OF SACRED DUTY

Jesus' Precept of Sacred Responsibility

———

"Unto whomsoever much is given,
of him shall much be required." Luke 12:48

Commonly, God is misunderstood or portrayed as a miser, a tyrant, or a grasper, who uses His omnipotence to extract any and all good that man possesses. This misperception is nearly always born from a father-wound, an affliction inflicted by a person who had won our affection, is our superior, or represents the goodness of God in some manner, but who has betrayed that trust. By inflicting the father-wound, the evil one, through the malice of a human being who represents God, convinces us that God cannot be trusted.

After inflicting the wound, Satan relentlessly manipulates and exacerbates this injury to increase an ever-deepening chasm between God and the human soul. This distrust, if left unchecked, metastasizes in the soul, convincing man that, because God is his enemy, he is not responsible to God, and, therefore, he avoids all spiritual responsibility.

Such a man believes that God has given him little, and, therefore, he has little to give God in return. He views God as a miser and, therefore, becomes miserly. He eventually, and disparagingly, accuses God of entrusting him with little, not realizing that it is because of his lack of trust in God that he has little.

In vain, man toils in his want for the ever-elusive "more," only to wallow in his self-pity of having less. Our Lord, however, wills for us to experience and possess the abundance of His life, joy, and peace, as indicated by His words, "The thief cometh not, but for to steal, and to kill, and to destroy. I am come that they may have life, and may have it more abundantly" (Jn 10:10). The Lord is clear that it is not God who takes, kills, dominates, and suppresses, but it is the evil one; it is God who purposes to afford man the superabundance of life.

To liberate man from Satan's false depiction of God the Father, our Lord Jesus imparts His wisdom, "for he that hath, to him shall be given, and he shall abound: but he that hath not, from him shall be taken away that also which he hath" (Mt 13:12).

Initially, Our Lord's words appear cryptic and unfair: To the one who has, to him more will be given, but to the one who has not, to him even the little he has will be taken away. This concept often conjures the impression that our Lord wants the rich to become richer, while He wills that the poor become poorer. Yet, this is a misreading and misunderstanding of Our Lord's wisdom.

Though human experience confirms the application of this principle in the material realm, and it does apply to temporal matters, Jesus is using the temporal to direct us to the supernatural.

It is true that those who are responsible with knowledge, investing in education, accumulate more knowledge; that those who are responsible with their wealth, investing their money, typically do increase their wealth; and that those who invest time in relationships often forge deep, enduring friendships. This principle, however, is especially applicable to the supernatural gifts and virtues such as wisdom, fortitude, purity, joy, peace, humility, faith, hope, and love.

When a man uses the gifts that he has received from God for God, his love of God and for God increases and, consequently, so also does his love for his neighbor. Whereas the man who squanders the gifts afforded to him loses even that which he had once possessed. For example, a man with strong muscle tone, who neglects to exercise, will experience the atrophying of his muscles. This principle also applies to the spiritual life. If a man neglects to use his gifts, he will certainly lose those gifts.

The harsh, bitter truth of the Gospel is that not everyone has a right to possess what others possess. The world's notion of human equality does not reflect Christ's truth of man's equal dignity. Contrary to socialistic or Marxist agendas, Jesus does not punish those who are gifted with more by robbing them of their talents and gifts for the purpose of supplying those who have less with more. This is robbery. Jesus expects man to be responsible with that which God has entrusted to him and to invest it, to grow it, to give it, and to be thankful for it.

As Jesus publicly proclaimed His Gospel, He shared with the crowds His parable of the Talents as a means to vividly depict the lesson of sacred responsibility. In the parable, the master, before departing on an extended journey, entrusted three servants with *his* talents: "And to one he gave five talents, and to another two, and to another one, to every one according to his proper ability" (Mt 25:15).

The master in the parable is a symbol of Christ Himself, who, prior to ascending to heaven, entrusted His Church and, in particular, every baptized Christian with the graces (symbolized by the talents) necessary to participate in saving souls. Jesus is fair. He never burdens us with unrealistic expectations that are beyond our God-given abilities but rather entrusts the gifts, talents, and graces that are in keeping with our nature.

As mentioned previously, a talent was a weight or measurement of Greek and Roman silver or gold that was the equivalent of a substantial amount of money—approximately nineteen years of wages, which indicates that the master was exceedingly generous and trusting.

When the master returned to settle accounts, the first servant came forward and demonstrated that he had doubled the five talents, and so also the second servant, who doubled his two talents. Yet, the third servant, who "going his way digged into the earth, and hid his lord's money" (Mt 25:18), "came and said: Lord, I know that thou art a hard man; thou reapest where thou has not sown, and gatherest where thou has not strewed. And being afraid I went and hid thy talent in the earth: behold here thou hast that which is thine" (Mt 25:24–25).

The perception that the third servant (also known as the wicked lazy servant) had of his master determined his actions and trajectory for his life. He perceived his master as being an uncompassionate, miserly, grasping tyrant, who took beyond what he gave. The wicked servant also expresses a sentiment that ought not to be glossed over: He feared his master, which indicates that he was a servile slave rather than a trusting son, and this fear debilitated his ability to serve. So, the master said, "Take ye away therefore the talent from him, and give it to him that hath ten talents" (Mt 25:28).

The challenging, two-fold lesson that Jesus is disclosing is, first, He increases the talents of those who invest the talents they have been entrusted with. Notice that the master did not take back the talents for himself, for he said, "Give it to him that hath ten talents." The master does not take for himself but only takes for the purpose of giving.

Second, if a man neglects to use his talent, he will most certainly lose it, and God will take that talent and give it to another who can be trusted to invest it. Again, Christ's Gospel runs contrary to the world and its maxims of equality. Jesus wills to liberate man from false equality so that he may live the fullness of his dignity, which is born from assuming sacred responsibility.

My son, with this lesson, Christ is counseling you to do two things: first, believe that you have received much from God our Father, which is expressed by your continual thanksgiving. Indeed, "be ye thankful" (Col 3:15), for gratitude gives birth to joy. Second, invest that which you have received from God by giving yourself in service to God and others. By doing so, God will multiply the gift in you that you may do greater things yet, for He promises "he that believeth in me, the works that I do, he also shall do; and greater than these" (Jn 14:12).

But woe to the man who believes that he has been given little, for the little he has will be removed from him and given to another, who with gratitude will invest it for Christ.

Lord Jesus, burn the image of your holy face into me
that I may become a revelation of your glory,
that I may proclaim as did the holy Apostle:
"It is no longer I who live, but Christ who lives in me." Amen.

Optional Scripture Readings: Matthew 25:14–30

FULFILL YOUR SELECTED SPIRITUAL PRACTICES FROM STAGE 3:
PRECEPTS AND PREPARATION.

Day 14

(Lent Week 2: Tuesday)

INVOCATION: JESUS, SHOW ME MY SINS,
THAT I MAY KNOW OF YOUR UNFATHOMABLE MERCY.

REAWAKENING HOPE

Jesus Discloses the Precept of Hope to the Samaritan Woman

"Give me to drink." John 4:7

Jesus and His disciples departed from Judea for Galilea, which was a three-day journey, that is, if a Jew was courageous enough to pass through Samaria (a territory situated between Judea and Galilee). Otherwise, circumventing Samaria would demand at least twice as much travel time.

"There was no deeper breach of human relations in the contemporary world than the feud of the Jews and Samaritans."[17] "To the Jews, the Samaritans were a heretical and schismatic group of spurious worshippers of the God of Israel, who were detested even

---

17   Geoffrey Chapman, *Dictionary of the Bible* London, Cassell and Collier Macmillan Publishers Ltd., 1976, 766.

more than the pagans."[18] Indeed, there was not a greater hostility than the 400-year schism between the Jews and Samaritans.

Nevertheless, as Jesus and His disciples traveled through Samaria, He became wearied from the journey and rested in Sychar, at a well that the patriarch Jacob, son of Isaac, had dug. While the disciples went into town to purchase food, a Samaritan woman came to the well to draw water; it was about noon—the sixth hour (see Jn 4:1–6).

"Jesus saith to her: Give me to drink" (Jn 4:7), to which she responded, "How dost thou, being a Jew, ask of me to drink, who am a Samaritan woman?" (Jn 4:9). Not only did an intensely hostile social barrier exist between Jews and Samaritans but also Jewish religious tradition forbade teachers to converse or even greet a woman in public.

Additionally, the women would fetch water from the well early in the morning, when it was cooler, to avoid the strenuous heat of the day, but this woman came to the well during the heat of the day, at the sixth hour, which discloses the stigma of her personal shame. Because of her sins, she is rejected by her own. This becomes evident when Jesus asked her to "go, call thy husband, and come hither" (Jn 4:16), to which she responded, "I have no husband" (Jn 4:17). Jesus then reveals her shame, "Thou hast said well, I have no husband: For thou hast had five husbands: and he whom thou now hast, is not thy husband" (Jn 4:17–18).

Nevertheless, Jesus refuses to allow religious strife, cultural difference, spiritual disciplines, or even the woman's shameful past to prevent Him from penetrating her soul with the hope of God's love for her. Indeed, Jesus' purpose of revealing His awareness of her

18   Ibid.

92

past to her is to awaken hope in her soul. This is expressed by His request, "Give me to drink" (Jn 4:7), which is another way of saying, "though you have been marginalized because of your sin, and live with shame, it is my wish to awaken you to your true dignity."

The Samaritan woman comes to draw water from Jacob's well— a symbol of the Torah, the Mosaic Law. Yet, Jesus explains that "whosoever drinketh of this water, shall thirst again" (Jn 4:13). In other words, the Law is incapable of quenching her thirst, or the thirst of any human being, for God, for holiness, or for sanctity— only Christ can satisfy, as He attests: "But he that shall drink of the water that I will give him, shall not thirst for ever: But the water that I will give him, shall become in him a fountain of water, springing up into life everlasting" (Jn 4:13–14).

This woman, who had been with six men—a symbol of the sixth day of creation on which man and beast alike were created— attempted to obtain a love that satisfies from creatures who cannot satisfy or be satisfied. Indeed, Christ now awakens within her, simultaneously, the reality that man, created on the sixth day, cannot satisfy her, and the hope that this seventh man, the perfect God-man, who sat before her, can fulfill her desire for love.

Again, Jesus exposed her sin to reveal to her that though men are unable to satiate her thirst for love, there is one who can: Jesus the Lord. Often man, burdened with the shame of his past, resorts to two remedies that are extreme polar opposites. On one hand, believing that his salvation is hopeless, he turns to creatures, repeatedly indulging his lusts and hoping to eventually quench his thirst for fulfillment. On the other hand, he turns to the well of the Law, or its modern version, believing that he can merit his own justification by a rigorous adherence to religious precepts, disciplines, devotions, and asceticism. Both so called "solutions" are ultimately man's way of ignoring his pathetic sinful condition.

But Christ desires to awaken hope within our souls by exposing our failed attempts to satiate our thirst for divine love. Christ alone can quench man's thirst for love—as demonstrated by the woman, who, after receiving Christ's words of hope, left her water jar empty at the well (see Jn 4:28).

Jesus had filled her with hope so that she no longer thirsted for false loves. In fact, Jesus' love liberates this woman from her shame, inspiring her to share her discovery that Jesus is the Christ with the people of her city, who also came to believe that He was the Christ because of her testimony (see Jn 4:31–42).

My son, your sin will prove to be no barrier to Christ who desires to awaken within you real hope that He alone can provide you the love that you cannot obtain from creatures. Christ thirsts for you to thirst for Him. Your response ought to be like this woman who said, "Sir, give me this water, that I may not thirst, nor come hither to draw" (Jn 4:15), meaning give me your Spirit, Lord, that I may never look to creatures to be satisfied. Give Him a little of your own love to drink, and He will quench your thirst with His love, a love that will compel you, like the Samaritan woman, to share it with others.

Lord Jesus, burn the image of your holy face into me
that I may become a revelation of your glory,
that I may proclaim as did the holy Apostle:
"It is no longer I who live, but Christ who lives in me." Amen.

+ JMJ +

Optional Scripture Readings: John 4:3-30

FULFILL YOUR SELECTED SPIRITUAL PRACTICES FROM STAGE 3: *PRECEPTS AND PREPARATION.*

Day 15

(Lent Week 2: Wednesday)

INVOCATION: JESUS, GIVE ME THE GRACE TO WORSHIP
THE FATHER IN SPIRIT AND IN TRUTH.

TRUE WORSHIP

Jesus Discloses the Precept of Worship to the Samaritan Woman

———————

"They that adore [God], must adore him in spirit
and in truth." John 4:24

Over the course of the last two millennia, Sacred Tradition
has developed and been enriched, liturgical devotions have
flourished, and personal disciplines have multiplied. The Catholic
Church, rich with traditions, gifted with a treasury of sacred liturgical rites, and stocked full of the most eloquent and emotionally
moving prayers of the saints and mystics, affords the faithful a wealth
of resources to aid in the worship of God and fuel devotion to Him.

Yet, far too often, the faithful Catholic focuses primarily on the
devotion or the discipline itself, while losing sight of the underlying
reason for the devotion, which must always be to foster and forge
communion with God and His Divine Will.

+ JMJ +

When the ultimate end of an intimate relational communion with God is eclipsed, man's motivation behind his prayers becomes tainted. Prayer becomes a method of attaining or extracting something, such as merit, from God.

Grace, "the *free and undeserved help* that God gives us to respond to his call to become children of God, adoptive sons, partakers of the divine nature and of eternal life" (CCC 1996), "is a *participation in the life of God*. It introduces us into the intimacy of Trinitarian life" (CCC 1997).

"The preparation of man for the reception of grace is already a work of grace. . . . God brings to completion in us what he also begun, 'since he who completes his work by cooperating with our will began by working so that we might will it'"[19] (CCC 2001).

The sacred liturgy, prayers of the saints and mystics, devotions and spiritual disciplines, Rosaries and chaplets, novenas, and the *Liturgy of the Hours* have been developed to serve as spiritual springboards that launch man into the depths of intimate communion, intimacy, and conversation with God.

Many, even among the faithful, mindlessly float upon the surface of preset pieties, presuming that such devotions will do for them that which they have neglected to do for themselves. Often, we become so dependent on the external form of the devotion that we neglect the internal spirit that validates them.

While resting at Jacob's well, during His conversation with the Samaritan woman, Jesus makes a statement that not only would alarm both Jew and Samaritan alike but is also shocking to those faithful of the Catholic Church that He established: "Believe me,

19   St. Augustine, *De gratia et libero arbitrio*, 17: PL 44,901.

that the hour cometh, when you shall neither on this mountain, nor in Jerusalem, adore the Father. ... But the hour cometh, and now is, when true adorers shall adore the Father in spirit and in truth. For the Father also seeketh such to adore him. God is a spirit; and they that adore him, must adore him in spirit and in truth" (Jn 4:21, 23–24).

The Jews and the Samaritans both had built their own temples on their own mountains as the central place of liturgical worship. Though each of these groups adhered to their religious traditions, particularly the Jews who had followed Moses' prescriptions for worship meticulously, Christ says of them, "This people honoureth me with their lips: but their heart is far from me" (Mt 15:8). In these words, we discover a hint to what Jesus means when He speaks of worshipping in spirit and in truth. Prayer must be from the heart and not the lips only.

St. Thomas Aquinas, reflecting on this matter, says that "two things are necessary for true worship: one is that the worship be spiritual: so [Jesus] says spirit, i.e., with a fervor of spirit: "I will pray with spirit, I will pray with my mind (1 Cor 14:15) singing to the Lord in your hearts (Eph 5:19)."[20] Notice that St. Thomas says that true worship engages both the mind and heart—it requires a fervent spirit.

"Second, the worship should be in truth. First in the truth of faith because no fervent spiritual desire is meritorious unless united to the truth of faith, 'ask with faith, without doubting' (Jas 1:6)."[21] "Second, truth, i.e., without pretense or hypocrisy; against such attitudes we read: They like to pray at street corners, so people can see them' (Mt

---

20 St. Thomas Aquinas, *Gospel of John Commentary*, 230.
21 Ibid.

6:5)."[22] True worship "requires three things: first, the fervor of love, second the truth of faith; and third a correct intention."[23]

Jesus, in His dialogue with the woman at the well, reveals the ultimate defining character that differentiates true worship from false empty devotion. Indeed, He makes the distinction between the slave and the spiritual son: "[Jesus] says 'the Father,' because under the Law, worship was not given to the Father, but to the Lord. We worship in love, as sons, whereas they worshipped in fear, as slaves."[24]

Filial love marked by trust in God is the hallmark of true worship. To worship in spirit and in truth is to worship God the Father in the Son, as the Son, through the Son. This is precisely why, in the final analysis, all religions other than Christianity ultimately fail; they are incapable of obtaining salvation from the Father, for they have not the Son of God who obtained salvation for man, and, for that reason, they have not the Father. Only God the Son can make men sons of God the Father. Jesus alone is the way to God the Father (see Jn 14:6), the refulgent truth of God the Father, and the fullness of God the Father's life (see Col 2:9). Without Christ, and sonship in Him, men are nothing more than slaves who worship God in fear rather than in love.

My son, Jesus asks you to examine your approach to worship. Do you pray with fervor and love? Or do you babble like the pagans, repeating prayers mindlessly? (see Mt 6:7) Do you pray and worship God in faith, trusting in His benevolence, or do you doubt His goodness? If you pray with doubt in your hearts, you have become an obstacle to your own prayers and sabotage your own requests.

22   Ibid.
23   Ibid.
24   Ibid., 231.

For this reason, fear is useless; what is needed is trust in God the Father (see Lk 8:50; Mk 5:36).

Lord Jesus, burn the image of your holy face into me
that I may become a revelation of your glory,
that I may proclaim as did the holy Apostle:
"It is no longer I who live, but Christ who lives in me." Amen.

Optional Scripture Readings: John 4:3–30; Matthew 6:1–13

FULFILL YOUR SELECTED SPIRITUAL PRACTICES FROM STAGE 3:
PRECEPTS AND PREPARATION.

Day 16

(Lent Week 2: Thursday)

INVOCATION: JESUS, GIVE ME THE GRACE TO
MAKE MY PRAYER EFFECTIVE.

TRUE POWER

The Transfiguration: Jesus Discloses the Precept of Powerful Prayer

———

"This kind can go out by nothing,
but by prayer and fasting." Mark 9:29

While atop Mount Tabor, Peter, James, and John become witnesses of Jesus' Transfiguration (see Mt 17). Our Lord's human countenance became resplendent in glory, bright as light, reflecting the reality of His divine nature. Centered between Moses, the human symbol of the Law, and Elijah, the human symbol of the prophets, Jesus is the integration, fullness, and fulfillment of both the Law and the prophets who foretold of Him.

As Jesus' inner circle of Apostles are awe stricken and confounded in ecstasy by the vision, God the Father Himself confirms that the Law and the prophets give way to the primacy of Jesus' teachings, "This is my beloved Son; hear him" (Lk 9:35). In this divine command,

God is mandating that we are to no longer appeal to the Law and the prophets, but to learn only from His Son who is the definitive fulfillment of both. In fact, the event of Jesus' Transfiguration is a symbol and foreshadowing of His triumphant resurrected glory. Considering this, Jesus' first action after His Transfiguration is also a symbol and foreshadowing of His mission to save souls after His Resurrection.

As Jesus, Peter, James, and John descended the mountain, they encountered a multitude engaged in a heated debate. The source of the contention was that Jesus' disciples were unable to cast out a demon from a boy, which provided the scribes and Pharisees the courage to vent their opposition to Jesus' disciples, identifying them as frauds.

Suddenly, the father of the possessed boy emerges from the crowd, and in desperation begged Jesus, "If thou canst do anything, help us, having compassion on us" (Mk 9:22). In hope and faith, the father had traveled some distance to obtain relief for his son and for his family. In the disciples, who had previously cast out demons, this father's hopes were not fulfilled but rather dashed. On the brink of despair, he begged Christ, "If thou canst do anything," meaning "your disciples could do nothing, can you do anything? Is this demon even beyond your power?" To which Jesus responded, "If thou canst believe, all things are possible to him that believeth. And immediately the father of the boy crying out, with tears said: I do believe, Lord: help my unbelief" (Mk 9:23–24).

Jesus after seeing that a crowd was gathering, quickly cast out the demon, returning the healed son to his faithful father. Our Lord's first miracle following the event of His Transfiguration was the healing of a possessed son—and not only the son, but the relationship between this son and his father, thus healing the father's family.

The evil one's strategy is to destroy the family, for it has been designed by God to be a living reflection of the self-giving, interpersonal love of the Triune God. To plunder the family, the devil sows division in marriage, which is a living symbol of Christ's fidelity to His bride, the Church. This division exacerbates the relationship between the human father and his children.

The symbolic implication of this event is that, after Christ's Resurrection, His evangelical mission will be founded upon the restoration of fatherhood in Christ, that the human father becomes an icon of the heavenly Father, and, thus, families will begin to reflect and relive the image of the Most Holy Trinity.

Ironically, as the Apostles and Christ descended Mount Tabor, the Apostles asked Him when Elijah would come, for God, through the prophet Malachi, had indicated that he must come prior to the coming of the Messiah: "Behold I will send you [Elijah] the prophet, before the great and dreadful day of the Lord. And he shall turn the heart of the fathers to the children, and the heart of the children to the fathers: lest I come, and strike the earth with anathema" (Mal 4:5–6).

In other words, a profound connection exists between the mission of Elijah and Christ's first miracle, which indicates God's intention and desire: to redeem and restore human fatherhood in the glory of God's fatherhood that the family may be redeemed in Christ and be a means of converting the nations to Christ, turning the hearts of fathers toward their children that children may turn to God the Father with trust in Him.

We discover an essential attribute of true, godly fatherhood in the father of this uplifting account: He deems his son's curse and ailment as his own, as testified by his words, "Help *us*, having compassion on *us!*" (Mk 9:22, emphasis added). This father, as any good father, bears his child's burdens as his own. Not only does he bear his child's burdens as his own, but he intercedes on his son's behalf, making tremendous sacrifices to bring him to Jesus. Indeed, in this father, we discover the mission of fatherhood: A father assumes sacrificial responsibility by gathering his family's burdens and needs and bringing them to Christ, interceding on their behalf.

But how is the human father to intercede for his family? Later, when Jesus' disciples ask Him privately why they could not cast out the demon, Christ explains that "this kind can go out by nothing, but by prayer and fasting" (Mk 9:29). In this brief statement, Christ provides us with the formula for prayer to have effective power and obtain the restoration of the family: prayer combined with, and fueled by, fasting—that is sacrifice on behalf of another—casts out evil and division.

So powerful is this truth that the evil one has convinced religious shepherds to remove this statement from the lectionary read at the Holy Sacrifice of the Mass in the Ordinary Form, so that it reads, "this kind can only be removed by prayer."[25] Indeed, prayer without fasting is lip service, and fasting without prayer is self-mastery. As with the soul and body, both prayer and sacrifice are necessary. The man who fasts demonstrates that he is willing to sacrifice himself for an altruistic desired outcome and that he believes what he prays and prays what he believes.

There exist three foundational components of friendship: trust, communication, and self-donation. By means of communication,

---

25 Some manuscripts add, "But this kind does not come out except by prayer and fasting," which is a variant of the better reading of Mk 9:29. [17:22–23] The second Passion prediction (cf. Mt 16:21–23) is the least detailed of the three and may be the earliest. Yet, the Greek text indicates that the word fasting is present in the text.

combined with self-donation, trust between persons is developed. If a man sacrifices for his wife, yet refuses to communicate with her, or if he communicates with his wife, yet neglects to sacrifice for her, their marriage will lack trust and intimacy, and will never achieve a full and mature expression of friendship and charity.

So it is in our friendship with God. Christ says, "I will not now call you servants . . . but I have called you friends" (Jn 15:15). Indeed, if our friendship with God is to express the full measure of charity, it is imperative that we communicate with God, which is prayer with fervor and love, and donate ourselves to God, which is sacrifice.

Secret sacrifice inspires and empowers our prayer, and prayer inspires us to sacrifice in secret. My son, this is power that defeats the devil and unites families in Christ.

Lord Jesus, burn the image of your holy face into me
that I may become a revelation of your glory,
that I may proclaim as did the holy Apostle:
"It is no longer I who live, but Christ who lives in me." Amen.

Optional Scripture Readings: Matthew 17:1–20; Mark 9:1–28; Malachi 4:5–6

FULFILL YOUR SELECTED SPIRITUAL PRACTICES FROM STAGE 3: *PRECEPTS AND PREPARATION.*

Day 17

(Lent Week 2: Friday)

INVOCATION: JESUS, GIVE ME THE GRACE TO
BE PERFECT AS YOUR FATHER IS PERFECT.

TRUE PERFECTION

*The Parable of the Good Samaritan:
Jesus Discloses the Precept of Perfection*

"Be you therefore perfect, as also your
heavenly Father is perfect." Matthew 5:48

Christian perfection can never be reduced to the mere absence of sin or a perfect adherence to religious precepts. Proof of this is Jesus Himself, who, though sinless and fulfilling the Law perfectly, pressed on toward ultimate human perfection. "Although he was a Son, he learned obedience through what he suffered; and being made perfect he became the source of eternal salvation for all who obey him" (Heb 5:8–9, RSV).

This does not indicate that Jesus lacked perfection at any point in His human life but that, at every stage of His life, He was perfectly obedient. The ultimate stage and finale of Christ's life was His sacrificial offering of Himself on the Cross. Jesus' example indicates that perfection, ultimately, is giving one's life in fulfillment of God's holy will. As the author of Hebrews says, "For you have not yet resisted unto blood, striving against sin" (Heb 12:4). Perhaps the most challenging and bold command Christ gave is "be you therefore perfect, as also your heavenly Father is perfect" (Mt 5:48). Often, when confronted with the daunting task of speaking to Christ's flock on this passage, preachers regard Jesus' words as hyperbole at best and an impossible command at worst. While it is true that no command of God can be fulfilled without the aid of grace, Christ does command us to fulfill that which is possible with His grace. How could Jesus demand such lofty sanctity from fallen human beings? How are we to interpret this command?

The key to interpreting Jesus' instruction regarding the matter of Christian perfection is to interpret His words in light of those preceding them:

> You have heard that it hath been said, Thou shalt love thy neighbor, and hate thy enemy. But I say to you, Love your enemies: do good to them that hate you: and pray for them that persecute you and calumniate you: That you may be children of your Father who is in heaven, who maketh his sun to rise upon the good, and bad, and raineth upon the just and unjust. For if you love them that love you, what reward shall you have? do not even the publicans this? And if you salute your brethren only, what do you more? do not also the heathens this'?" (Mt 5:43–47).

Jesus' words indicate that perfection consists in being like God the Father who loves all His children—those who are faithful and those who are rebellious—willing that all be saved (see 1 Tm 2:4).

Though the entire life of Jesus Christ is testimony to this truth, He conveys this reality powerfully and provocatively in His parable of the Good Samaritan, which was His response to a scribe's question: "Who is my neighbour?" (Lk 10:29).

A certain man went down from Jerusalem to Jericho, and fell among robbers, who also stripped him, and having wounded him went away, leaving him half dead. . . . A certain priest went down the same way: and seeing him, passed by. In like manner also a Levite, when he was near the place and saw him, passed by. But a certain Samaritan being on his journey, came near him; and seeing him, was moved with compassion. And going up to him, bound his wounds, pouring in oil and wine. (Lk 10:30–34)

The priest and the Levite were among the most respected Jews. A Levite was a member of the tribe of Levi, whose role was to assist the priests in worship in the Jewish Temple. For the Levite and priest, perfection was synonymous with the meticulous fulfillment of the prescriptions of the Law of Moses.

In the situation that Jesus' proposes in this parable, both the Levite and the priest would have been highly concerned about obeying the Law, which stated that if any man touch a dead body, he was unclean for seven days (see Nm 19:11), thus barring them both from Temple service—a most prestigious work.

Additionally, there existed the possibility that the man half-dead was a Gentile, or could have been touched by a Gentile during the assault, rendering him, and any who touched him, unclean, meaning again that the priest and Levite would surrender their privileged Temple service.

By highlighting the characters of the priest and Levite in His parable, Jesus demonstrates that perfection is not the mere fulfillment of religious precepts regarding liturgical worship, but rather the sacrifice and offering of self, even for one who is identified as an enemy or as having a set of beliefs that run contrary to our own. In fact, Jesus intentionally uses the figure of the Samaritan as the ideal of compassion, as the man of perfection, as an indictment against the person who reduces love of God and religious perfection to the fulfillment of legal prescriptions and practices. Indeed, the Jew, because of the gift of the Law, believed himself chosen and righteous, while believing that the Samaritan was condemned.

Additionally, and repeatedly, the early Church Fathers interpreted the man who fell among brigands, was stripped of his clothing, and left half-dead as Adam and the sons of Adam, who, after falling into sin, irrevocably left paradise (symbolized by Jerusalem), taking the road to perdition (symbolized by the road to Jericho), whereupon he was assaulted by Satan (symbolized by the brigands), who stripped him of his dignity as a son of God (symbolized by the stripping of his clothing), thus leaving him half-dead (a figure of the man who has lost the likeness of God). The term half-dead indicates that even though sin had removed man's likeness to God, yet a spark of God's image remained within him. He was not, as Martin Luther proposed, "utterly depraved," which would indicate that the man would be completely spiritually dead.

Considering this, the good Samaritan is a rich symbol of Jesus Himself, who associated Himself with a foreigner—a Samaritan. He, the outcast, the reviled one, is the one who anoints the wounds of the sinner with the grace afforded by the sacraments (symbolized by the wine and oil), handing him over to the Church (symbolized by the innkeeper), imparting to him Christ's human dignity and divine image (as symbolized by the two coins).

After concluding His parable, Jesus asked the lawyer that tested Him, and asks us, "Which of these three, in thy opinion, was neighbour to him that fell among robbers?" (Lk 10:36), to which the lawyer replied, "He that shewed mercy to him. And Jesus said to him: Go, and do thou in like manner" (Lk 10:37).

My son, Christian perfection does not consist in the mere fulfillment of religious precepts but in extending charity to one's neighbor and even to one's enemies. Go and do likewise.

Lord Jesus, burn the image of your holy face into me
that I may become a revelation of your glory,
that I may proclaim as did the holy Apostle,
"It is no longer I who live, but Christ who lives in me." Amen.

Optional Scripture Readings: Matthew 5:38–48; Luke 10:25–37

FULFILL YOUR SELECTED SPIRITUAL PRACTICES FROM STAGE 3:
PRECEPTS AND PREPARATION.

Day 18

(Lent Week 2: Saturday)

INVOCATION: JESUS, GIVE ME THE GRACE TO
KEEP HOLY THE LORD'S DAY.

THE SIGN OF THE SON

Jesus' Precept of Rest

"The sabbath was made for man,
and not man for the sabbath." Mark 2:27

The ultimate proof that one is an adopted son of God is his unfailing trust in God the Father. In the modern age, one of the most challenging, misunderstood, and, perhaps, forgotten applications of this filial trust is keeping holy the Lord's Day.

Unfortunately, many men view Sunday as a day to "catch up" on the work they were unable to complete during the previous week—a day to accrue more money, a day to increase the value of their property, a day to "get ahead" on work, or a day to engage in meaningless, mind-numbing entertainment.

Experience demonstrates that quite often men who work on Sunday remain in their pitiful, stressful situation, riddled by lack of time, lack of resources, lack of peace, and lack of regenerative rest. By keeping Sunday for himself, man does not keep the Lord's Day holy, nor does he keep himself holy.

Keeping the Lords' Day holy offers a man the opportunity to express two things: first, his gratitude for God's provision during the previous week and, second, his faith that God will continue to provide during the following week. The Lord's Day affords man the opportunity to reflect on the fact that God is trustworthy, which inspires him to trust God more deeply.

The Law of the Sabbath rest (keeping the Lord's Day holy) is a sign of God's covenant with His people. The ultimate sign of the New Covenant is Christ's Holy Sacrifice of the Mass, the Eucharist, which He, through His priests, offers precisely within the context of the Lord's Day.

On the Lord's Day, amidst the Holy Sacrifice of the Mass, an exchange between God and man occurs: Christ gives man His Body and Blood—the Eucharistic sacrifice—and man gives himself to God, expressed by his giving the Lord's Day to God as his sacrifice.

Yet, this donation of Sunday to God cannot be reduced to "not working." Again, perfection does not consist in an absence of evil but rather a fullness of goodness (not that work is evil, but rather servile work on Sunday is). Therefore, rest per se is not a fulfillment of the command to keep the Lord's Day holy.

The Jewish interpretation of the Law regarding the Sabbath had become so strict that the letter of Law became an opposition to the spirit behind the Law given by God. This is evident in the account of Jesus' healing of the woman with a crippled spirit.

And [Jesus] was teaching in their synagogue on their sabbath. And behold there was a woman, who had a spirit of infirmity eighteen years: and she was bowed together, neither could she look upwards at all. Whom when Jesus saw, he called her unto him, and said to her: Woman, thou art delivered from thy infirmity. And he laid his hands upon her, and immediately she was made straight, and glorified God. And the ruler of the synagogue (being angry that Jesus had healed on the sabbath) answering, said to the multitude: Six days there are wherein you ought to work. In them therefore come, and be healed; and not on the sabbath day. And the Lord answering him, said: Ye hypocrites, doth not every one of you, on the sabbath day, loose his ox or his ass from the manger, and lead them to water? And ought not this daughter of Abraham, whom Satan hath bound, lo, these eighteen years, be loosed from this bond on the sabbath day? (Lk 13:10–16)

And [Jesus] said to them: The sabbath was made for man, and not man for the sabbath. (Mk 2:27)

The Gospel writer, St. Luke, is careful to mention that this woman was crippled by her infirmity for eighteen years. The number eighteen is comprised of the sum of three sixes, indicating the number of the beast: 666. Luke emphasizes this point by stating that the woman could not look upwards at all, a figure of one not being able to praise the God of heaven. Indeed, the evil one was binding her in his curse that she may not give glory to God. This is confirmed by Jesus Himself, who referred to her as a "daughter of Abraham, whom Satan hath bound, lo, these eighteen years."

Christ mentions that this woman is a "daughter of Abraham," which indicates that He had identified her as a symbolic figure of all of Israel, the "daughter of Abraham."

This account expresses that rigid, law-abiding sabbath rest, while neglecting to be charitable to one's neighbor, is a mark of the beast.

The sabbath rest was created by God not only to free man from constant toil and to trust in Him, but also that man might do the charitable works of God that help to liberate man from his sufferings.

In fact, on another occasion, when Jesus had healed a crippled man on the sabbath, the Jews sought to "persecute Jesus, because he did these things on the sabbath. But Jesus answered them: My Father worketh until now; and I work" (Jn 5:16–17).

In the beginning, God created man on the sixth day with the beasts, intending for man to live with Him on the seventh day. The seventh day was noted as the day that God "rested" form all His work. God commands every man to imitate and participate in His divine example by resting from servile work, the pursuit of mammon, and slavery to material and temporal matters.

Yet, God through Jesus, summons man to keep holy the Lord's Day by doing what the Lord does: extending charity to one's neighbor. This is confirmed by the fact that when Jesus said, "My Father worketh until now; and I work. Hereupon therefore the Jews sought the more to kill [Jesus], because he did not only break the sabbath, but also said God was his Father, making himself equal to God" (Jn 5:17–18). Not only did Jesus claim to be God, but, as God, He reclaimed the sabbath rest as a day to do good.

The intention of the ultimate beast, the devil, is to drive man to spend his life consuming and being consumed by the world. When man labors for wages, carries out his own pursuits, and neglects to commune with God on the Lord's Day, he becomes a slave to Satan, a beast burdened by the Beast; he incurs a curse rather than a blessing.

Yet, God does indeed desire to bless man. The Lord grants man the Lord's Day not only that he may rest from his labors, but also that he may liberate others from their labors.

Often a man protests the command of the sabbath rest by saying that he enjoys working. Yet, nowhere does God command that we do that which is agreeable on the sabbath, but he does say through the prophet, "If thou turn away thy foot from the sabbath, *from doing thy own will* in my holy day, and call the sabbath delightful, and the holy of the Lord glorious, and glorify him, *while thou dost not thy own ways,* and thy own will is not found: to speak a word: Then shalt thou be delighted in the Lord, and I will lift thee up above the high places of the earth. . . . For the mouth of the Lord hath spoken it" (see Is 58:13–14, emphasis added).

A son who generously sacrifices by keeping the Lord's Day holy, holy will the Lord make that man, and he shall delight in the Lord, and the Lord shall delight in him.

Lord Jesus, burn the image of your holy face into me
that I may become a revelation of your glory,
that I may proclaim as did the holy Apostle,
"It is no longer I who live, but Christ who lives in me." Amen.

Optional Scripture Readings: Luke 13:10–17; John 5:16–27

FULFILL YOUR SELECTED SPIRITUAL PRACTICES FROM STAGE 3:
PRECEPTS AND PREPARATION.

Stage 4

Third Week of Lent

SUMMONS TO SACRIFICIAL RESPONSIBILITY

During this fourth stage of our Lenten journey, we follow Christ as He reveals the key central tenant of the Christian man's life: sacrifice. At this point in Christ's journey—our journey—we encounter the perplexing paradoxical nature of the Cross. Indeed, Jesus reveals to us that we are to live to die, that the shame of the Cross is His and our glory, that the repelling pain of sacrifice is magnetic and conquers the sin of isolation, that thanksgiving—precisely for the Cross—is true worship, and that the world, the flesh, and devil will never cease tempting man to avoid the scandal of the Cross for the purpose of keeping him from attaining his ultimate glory. Indeed, Christ reveals to us our sacred responsibility that is always connected with His Cross. By means of committing ourselves to daily, hidden sacrifices, while maintaining our prayer devotions and silencing the kingdom of noise as transmitted by smart phones, social media, and television, we avail ourselves to God's grace that empowers our prayer and makes it truly effective.

STAGE 4 SPIRITUAL PRACTICES
(SELECT TWO OR THREE)

The purpose of this stage is to develop a spirit of sacrifice that fosters a sense of courage and increases our capacity to become responsible for those who are entrusted to us. Prayer becomes powerful when supported and animated by sacrifice. Only a leader who sacrifices himself and his selfish will is worthy of being followed.

+ JMJ +

———————

Make one daily hidden sacrifice.

———————

Reduce all forms of social media.

———————

Give up your phone during family time.

———————

Do not look at the phone, emails, social media, or news until after morning prayer.

———————

Do not look at the phone, emails, social media, or news after evening prayer.

———————

Limit yourself to one movie or television program per week.

———————

Do not listen to music or news while in car.

Day 19

(Lent Week 3: Sunday)

Invocation: Jesus, give me the grace to be thankful.

The Desirable Sacrifice

The Cleansing of the Lepers: The Sacrifice of Thanksgiving

———

"Were not ten made clean? and where are
the nine?" Luke 17:17

Among the greatest challenges posed to man is that he be consistently generous. With difficulty, one may give from abundance, but far more challenging it is to give from a position of want and need.

Man often gives because of coercion, guilt, *quid pro quo*, or the desire to establish business partnerships, win friends, or gain recognition and honor. When these are absent, there remain only two true motivations that inspire a man to be generous: another's dire need (to be compassionate) and gratitude, and, when giving altruistically, the two are one.

When a man is grateful for that which he has received, he is compelled to give to others in their need. He who believes that God has given much to him will give much in return to God. Indeed, the grateful man gives to others generously as God in His generosity has given to him.

It is not necessarily true that the more one has, the more one gives. Unfortunately, man becomes attached to, and dependent on, what he possesses and, therefore, lives in the continual fear of losing that which he possesses. This fear blinds him to the fact that God has dealt generously with him. Fear is like a type of spiritual rust that rots the soul's memory of God's providence.

The core of all sin is a lack of trust in God, which manifests itself in a negligence or denial of God's providence, which consequentially manifests itself in the behavior of ingratitude. Such ingratitude leads to selfishness, miserliness, hoarding, and the belief that we and our accomplishments are "self-made." When God commands the self-made man to offer a sacrifice of thanksgiving, he becomes resentful toward God, deeming Him as a taker.

Jesus's parable of the Husbandman powerfully expresses how the evil of ingratitude eventually leads to hostility toward God. A man "planted a vineyard, and made a hedge round about it, dug in it a press, and built a tower, and let it out to husbandmen; and went into a strange country. And when the time of [the harvest] drew nigh, he sent his servants to the husbandmen that they might receive the fruits thereof" (Mt 21:33–34). But they, who were stewards of the vineyard, beat, killed, and stoned the vineyard owners' messengers. Last of all, the owner sent his son whom they "cast forth out of the vineyard, and killed" (Mt 21:39).

The owner of the vineyard is a symbol of God the Father, who endows man with the vineyard, a symbol of creation over which God grants man dominion. The hedge is a symbol of God's protection.

The vat, or wine press, where the grapes are crushed for the purpose of obtaining the juice, which would ferment and become wine, is a symbol of man's temporal works that, if given to God, can be transformed into grace (symbolized by wine).

God desires that man offer to God a sacrifice of thanksgiving that God may use what man gives and transform his efforts into grace for mankind. This is the sacrifice of thanksgiving that the psalmist refers to: "The one who offers thanksgiving as his sacrifice glorifies me" (Ps 50:23, ESV).

It is important to note that the Greek word for eucharist (*eucharistia*) means thanksgiving and that the core root word for eucharist is *charis*, which is rendered in the vernacular as grace. God grants man the many and varied fruits of creation.

Man attends the liturgy of the Eucharistic sacrifice and offers his sacrifice of thanksgiving—in union with Christ's thanksgiving sacrifice—for the many graces he has received from God. Man again receives grace in this Most Blessed Sacrament. The Eucharist is an exchange between God and man: Our Lord gives grace (*charis*) in His Eucharist, and we receive this grace (*charis*), giving thanksgiving (*eucharistia*) in return.

The dynamic of reception of grace and returning thanksgiving for the grace received is vividly portrayed in the account of Jesus' healing of the ten lepers. As Jesus and His disciples passed through Samaria, they encountered ten men, ravaged and plagued by the disease of leprosy, who begged Jesus to have mercy upon them.

Jesus said to them, "Go, shew yourselves to the priests. And it came to pass, as they went, they were made clean. And one of them, when he saw that he was made clean, went back, with a loud voice glorifying God. And he fell on his face before [Jesus'] feet, giving thanks: and this was a Samaritan. And Jesus answering, said, Were not ten made clean? and where are the nine?... Arise, go thy way; for thy faith hath made thee whole'" (Lk 17:14–17, 19).

Though all ten lepers were healed, only the Samaritan was made whole. Once again, Jesus highlights that worshipping in spirit has priority over religious affiliation and legal prescriptions. While the nine may have fulfilled the prescription of the Law, "show thyself to the priest," only the "stranger," the outcast, the non-Jew, returned— without presenting himself to a priest—to give Jesus thanks.

A man who worships in spirit and in truth cannot rely solely on his religious affiliation or on religious disciplines. Though these are necessary, his devotion must be motivated by heartfelt thanksgiving.

Often, men frequent the sacraments without the disposition of heartfelt gratitude to God for the graces He has bestowed. To partake in the Eucharistic sacrifice without a spirit of thanksgiving is to receive Christ's sacrifice unworthily. Indeed, a man who receives the Eucharist while being ungrateful, or even selfish, can endanger his soul. As St. Paul says, "For he that eateth and drinketh unworthily, eateth and drinketh judgment to himself, not discerning the body of the Lord" (1 Cor 11:29). To discern the Lord's presence in the Most Blessed Sacrament is to discern His Body and Blood, which is His thanksgiving offering to the Father. Discernment of Christ's thanksgiving demands that a man be thankful in Christ.

To worship as Jesus is to live a Eucharistic life, wherein we praise God for the daily grace (*charis*) received, which is expressed by making a return to Him of what we already have received.

Truly, the acceptable sacrifice is the sacrifice of thanksgiving (see Ps 50:23) for it liberates man from slavery to the fear of losing that which he possesses. The sacrifice of thanksgiving enables man to delight in God, for, by thanking God, man discovers the goodness of the Father.

Therefore, my son, return to Jesus, thanking Him for the grace (*charis*) you have received, and, in receiving the Eucharist, offer yourself—in union with Christ—as a thanksgiving sacrifice to God the Father. This is your spiritual worship.

> *Lord Jesus, burn the image of your holy face into me*
> *that I may become a revelation of your glory,*
> *that I may proclaim as did the holy Apostle:*
> *"It is no longer I who live, but Christ who lives in me." Amen.*

Optional Scripture Reading: Luke 17:11–19; Matthew 21:33–43

FULFILL YOUR SELECTED SPIRITUAL PRACTICES FROM STAGE 4: *SUMMONS TO SACRIFICIAL RESPONSIBILITY.*

Day 20

(Lent Week 3: Monday)

INVOCATION: JESUS, GIVE ME THE GRACE TO
OVERCOME ISOLATION AND DESIRE COMMUNION.

THE SIN OF ISOLATION

The Grain of Wheat: Sacrifice that Conquers Loneliness

"Unless the grain of wheat falling into the ground die,
Itself remaineth alone." John 12:24–25

It is a great paradox that the men who are often most admired are those who are most lonely. Noticed and renowned for their popularity, they remain unknown for who they really are. They scale the heights of notoriety, which restricts them from being associated with the lowly. This was the plight of the Pharisee: In his aspiration and pursuit of holiness, he separated himself from sinners, and, by doing so, he could not minister to them, which would have aided him in becoming holy.

The man aspiring for holiness can be duped into believing that he must appear perfect to be attractive. Yet, it is this apparent perfection that often distances himself from others and others from himself. His persona of holiness, rather than attracting sinners to God, convinces sinners that God is repelled by their sins. An inability to lower oneself and associate with the lowly breeds isolation.

After Jesus' triumphal entry into Jerusalem, He was told by Andrew and Philip that certain Gentiles longed to visit with Him. Jesus responded by saying, "The hour is come, that the Son of man should be glorified. Amen, amen I say to you, unless the grain of wheat falling into the ground die, Itself remaineth alone" (Jn 12:23–25).

Initially, the two elements of the Gentiles longing to see Jesus and Christ's words of the dying grain of wheat have little connection. However, after closer inspection, we discover that Jesus is warning His Apostles that His ministry is not about public opinion and favorability. It is as if Philip and Andrew are expressing to Jesus their enthusiasm that even the Gentiles now wish to follow Him. Yet, as St. Paul says about Christ crucified, it is "unto the Jews indeed a stumbling block, and unto the Gentiles foolishness: But unto them that are called, both Jews and Greeks, Christ the power of God, and the wisdom of God" (1 Cor 1:23–24). In other words, Jesus' ministry will not become popular, for it always involves the Cross.

Jesus has now turned His gaze towards His final end—His Crucifixion. In this moment, Christ was awakening the Apostles to the reality that regardless of current popular favor, both Gentile and Jew will reject the shame of the Cross.

Jesus is adamant that His mission, and the mission of the Christian man, must end with death to self—self-donation for the salvation of souls; otherwise, he will, in the end, be alone, which from the divine perspective is not good. "It is not good for man to be alone" (Gen 2:18). Notice that Jesus does not equate popularity with communion, but rather self-donation with communion. Ironically, one can be popular and remain alone.

The grain of wheat is a symbol of the human being, who, by falling to the ground, a symbol of lowering oneself to serve others, plants the seed of charity in the world around him that it may rise and bear fruit. Yet, if the grain of wheat refuses to lower itself, it remains alone, never achieving true divine and human companionship.

Christian perfection cannot be reduced to the appearance of being a perfect Christian. Holiness is wholeness. Communion with God, through solitude with God, must bear the fruit of communion with others by the habitual act of serving others. If a man intentionally isolates himself from others, it is a certain sign, regardless of how much he prays, that he has isolated himself from God.

While the interior life is primary and indispensable, the temptation to reduce Christian holiness to the interior life of self-control, asceticism, and devotional and liturgical adherence is understandable. Solitude with God has the appearance of making God manageable, and predictable devotions convince us that God is predictable. Indeed, in the circumstances of personal prayer and devotions, man deviates little in his devotion, for he determines the length, duration, and form.

To approach the spiritual life in this manner creates a false dichotomy of service without prayer or prayer without service. Service without prayer is to act without being commanded by God. Prayer without service is to be commanded by God, yet to take no action.

Inherent to and associated with engaging other fallen human beings with the intention to inject Jesus' love into their lives is the risk of an unpredictable outcome, which can result in misunderstandings, tensions, and personal rejection.

Considering this, man often avoids sharing Jesus and His Gospel with others. He reduces his relationship with God to his prayer life, and, by doing so, he inadvertently shapes God into his image rather than allowing God to shape and re-create him to God's image.

If a man neglects to donate himself in service to others, he will, in the end, become a lonely, isolated, unloving, and unlovable man. The level to which one gives is the measure that will be given unto him, and the degree to which one loves is the level that he will receive.

Indeed, it is far easier to avoid attempting to achieve Christian communion with others, to live in isolation, and to suffer loneliness than to overcome loneliness and isolation for the purpose of bringing Christ's life to others.

Jesus Himself often rose early in the morning venturing into places of solitude to be alone with His Father. Yet, on a daily basis, He wandered and lived among broken men whom He identified as His Apostles. The fruit of Jesus' solitude with God was His consistent service to others for the purpose of bringing God's presence to them. To become unconquerable, the Christian man must embrace the paradoxical truth: Solitude with God leads to communion with others. Indeed, by spending his life for others, man will truly live.

As Jesus says, "But if [the grain of wheat] die, it bringeth forth much fruit" (Jn 12:25). Indeed, "loneliness opposes love. On the borderline of loneliness, love must become suffering."[26]

My son, it is imperative that you move from the world of isolation and loneliness, across the threshold and frontier of suffering, for the purpose of bringing Christ's presence to those around you.

---

26 Karol Wojtyla, *Radiation of Fatherhood*, https://donboscosalesianportal.org/wp-content/uploads/Radiation_of_Fatherhood.pdf.

Christ received must always lead to Christ given; otherwise, we remain alone, now and for all eternity.

Lord Jesus, burn the image of your holy face into me
that I may become a revelation of your glory,
that I may proclaim as did the holy Apostle:
"It is no longer I who live, but Christ who lives in me." Amen.

Optional Scripture Readings: John 12:23–33

FULFILL YOUR SELECTED SPIRITUAL PRACTICES FROM STAGE 4:
SUMMONS TO SACRIFICIAL RESPONSIBILITY.

Day 21

(Lent Week 3: Tuesday)

TRUE GLORY

Magnetic Self-Sacrifice

"And I, if I be lifted up from the earth,
will draw all things to myself." John 12:32

D aily, the Church's faithful, prior to the rising of the sun, at the very beginning of each day's prayer, pray the Invitatory (Psalm 95), which precedes either the Office of Readings or the Morning Prayer in the Liturgy of the Hours, It is called the Invitatory or Invitatory Psalm because it is not only an invitation to praise God but also an invitation to hearken and believe in Him.

The psalm invites us to recall the Israelites wandering in the desert, when their faith in God and His servant Moses faltered, and they grumbled and complained bitterly against the Lord:

Today, listen to the voice of the Lord: Do not grow stubborn, as your fathers did in the wilderness, when at Meriba and Massah they challenged me and provoked me, Although they had seen all of my works. Forty years I endured that generation, I said, "They are a people whose hearts go astray, and they do not know my ways." So I swore in my anger, "They shall not enter into my rest." (Ps 95:7–11, Liturgy of the Hours).

The Church, through the psalmist, summons us to hearken to the voice of the Lord rather than committing the same transgression of the Israelites. Repeatedly, the Chosen People of God, after witnessing His miraculous interventions and provisions, vented their anger against Him.

Grumbling or complaining against God incurs divine punishment because one who grumbles ignores that which God has provided generously and, rather than being thankful for His provisions, focuses on that which has not yet been given.

On one occasion, after God miraculously delivered the Canaanites into the Israelites hands, allowing them to destroy all of their cities, the People of God "began to be weary of their journey and labour: and [spoke] against God and Moses" (Nm 21:4–5). "Wherefore the Lord sent among the people fiery serpents, which bit them and killed many of them. Upon which they came to Moses, and said: We have sinned, because we have spoken against the Lord and thee: pray that he may take away these serpents from us. . . . . And the Lord said to [Moses]: Make a brazen serpent, and set it up for a sign: whosoever being struck shall look on it, shall live" (Nm 21:6–8).

Amidst His conversation with Andrew and Philip, regarding His determination to embrace His destiny of the Cross, Jesus tells them, "And I, if I be lifted up from the earth, will draw all things to myself" (Jn 12:32). "As Moses lifted up the serpent in the desert, so must the Son of man be lifted up" (Jn 3:14).

The serpent, which was a cause of death to the Israelites, is a figure of "the serpent," the devil himself, who is given permission to torture those who rebel against God. Yet, God through Moses, commanded that a serpent of bronze be raised on a staff that all who look upon it may be healed. This bronze serpent is a symbol of Christ, who embodying all sinful men, particularly Adam, who was the cause of our Fall, is lifted up on the Cross, that all who look upon Him with belief, trust, and gratitude may be healed.

The Greek word for "lifted up" (*hypsoō*), which was used by our Lord on three occasions (see John 3; 8; 12), can be interpreted as being lifted up in execution or being lifted up in exaltation. The fact that Jesus used this word interchangeably indicates that He equates His Crucifixion with His exaltation—the two are one. Once again, Jesus' Gospel is paradoxical: What appears most abject, reprehensible, scornful, and disgraceful—the Cross—is Christ's glory.

The world's concept of glory is in clear opposition to divine logic. Triumphant suffering, heroic sacrifice, the faithful endurance of persecution, and living a life of gratitude amidst heartache—offered to God for souls—is to be lifted up in glory. The Christian paradox of self-giving proclaims that such wounds, as Christ's wounds, will be eternally glorified.

Jesus offered Himself, without complaint, embracing the scourge of the Cross and, by doing so, became a magnet of glory that is capable of drawing all men to Himself. And, by offering yourself and your bodily, spiritual, and emotional sufferings to God in union with Christ without complaint, you will become a magnet of self-giving love.

Jesus' words demand a radical mind-shift: Our exaltation will only occur if we are lifted up (*hypsoō*) from slavery to comforts and disordered attachments. Gratitude that leads to self-donation, rather than grumbling, is the path to a life of freedom in Christ.

My son, there exists a direct correlation between the level of your sacrificial love and the level of your exaltation. Have faith, therefore, and believe that God wills to lift you up (*hypsoō*) and to exalt you.

Lord Jesus, burn the image of your holy face into me
that I may become a revelation of your glory,
that I may proclaim as did the holy Apostle:
"It is no longer I who live, but Christ who lives in me." Amen.

Optional Scripture Readings: Numbers 21:5–9; John 3:13–18

FULFILL YOUR SELECTED SPIRITUAL PRACTICES FROM STAGE 4:
SUMMONS TO SACRIFICIAL RESPONSIBILITY.

Day 22

(Lent Week 3: Wednesday)

INVOCATION: JESUS, TEACH ME TO BE A LEADER
WORTHY OF BEING FOLLOWED.

THE SHEPHERD AND THE HIRELING

The Self-Sacrificial Leader

"The good shepherd giveth his life for his sheep." John 10:11

Common among tribal cultures and ancient civilizations were rites of passage by which a boy endured formal testing, often through severe and dangerous methods, by men of his community for the purpose of him being acknowledged by society as a man.

Though these customs and rites have nearly disappeared from modern society, men continuously prove themselves by testing their mettle and courage, pressing their bodily and mental endurance, and pushing to the limits of their physical strength.

This testing is an echo of an inherent, innate need to be known and to know that the boy truly has become a man. Though the need for validation in the masculine soul remains, man has become deafened as to the reason for the rite. Because of this, many variants of pseudo-masculine rites—having the character of the ridiculous and meaningless (consider gang and fraternity initiations)—repeatedly surface. Originally, the rite of passage, and being received as a man by men, was never intended to be the end goal.

Beyond the superficial desire of being "included" as a man among men, male rites of passage serve the singular, noble purpose of preparing the boy for sacrificial responsibility. Though rites of passage may include actions such as hunting, fighting, or working, these challenges are not the final end but rather are a means to instill confidence, knowledge, patience, and grit in the boy that he may eventually protect, provide, and lead others—even sacrificing his life for those whom he has become responsible.

The rite is a remedy that attempts to resolve the perennial problem of a boy who habitually avoids suffering at all cost and depends on others to be responsible for himself while taking no responsibility. The end purpose of a true rite of passage is to "transform" the boy into a spiritual father—a man who becomes responsible not only for himself but for others, which gives him the impetus and courage to embrace tremendous sufferings and sacrifices.

Unfortunately, in our modern age, it is more common that men are merely boys trapped in men's bodies—hirelings who avoid suffering that does not directly benefit themselves. Bound by their own initiatives and self-indulgence, they flee from real sacrifice because such sacrifice demands a loss of something dear to the one offering it.

The true man, the spiritual father, deems his goods, his self-preservation, his comforts as rubbish in comparison to the life of those for whom he is responsible. This constitutes the real man: He gives of himself and that which he holds dear that others may have a better life—even life itself—and, particularly, and ultimately, life eternal.

David, the second king of Israel, became such a man. At one point, while yet a young shepherd boy, his father Jesse commanded him to bring food provisions to his brothers who were camped out at war against the Philistines. When the ruddy youth arrived at the camp, he discovered the host of the Israelite army cowered, huddled in hiding from Goliath, a great warrior, who repeatedly challenged any Israelite to confront him in hand-to-hand combat. Goliath's proposal was that the winner would take all and subject the entirety of the other nation to the victor and his people.

Seized with righteous indignation, and inspired by God, David approached King Saul requesting that he be granted permission to do combat with the giant who repeatedly blasphemed Israel's God. Saul rebuked the shepherd boy, "Thou art not able to withstand this Philistine, nor to fight against him: for though art but a boy, but he is a warrior from his youth" (1 Sm 17:33).

David responded, "Thy servant kept his father's sheep, and there came a lion, or a bear, and took a ram out of the midst of the flock: And I pursued after them, and struck them, and delivered it out of their mouth: and they rose up against me, and I caught them by the throat, and I strangled and killed them" (1 Sm 17:34–35).

Notice that Saul sees David as a boy, but David, having endured many rites of passage—assuming responsibility and risking his life for his father's flocks—has a real confidence and certain knowledge that he is a man. Indeed, by enduring these trials and tests, David was ready to assume responsibility for Israel's soldiers, women, and children by confronting the warrior giant, who he eventually struck down, thus routing the Philistines.

Jesus Christ, the Son of David (see Mt 1:1; Mt 12:23; Mt 15:22; Mt 21:9; Mk 10:48; Jn 7:42; Rm 1:3; 2 Tm 2:8; Rev 5:5), a typological fulfillment of the shepherd boy David, proclaimed, "I am the good shepherd. The good shepherd giveth his life for his sheep" (Jn 10:11).

Jesus, like David, who took on wild beasts, will take on the ultimate beast, confronting the devil and death for the purpose of liberating His sheep who have become trapped in the devil's grasp. Christ confirms that His battle is with the evil one: "The thief [the devil] cometh not, but for to steal, and to kill, and to destroy. I am come that they may have life, and may have it more abundantly" (Jn 10:10).

Our Lord draws a distinction between the shepherd and the hireling for the purpose of demonstrating to His Apostles who He is, as opposed to the religious leaders who are hirelings, while also giving His Apostles a vision of what they are to become: "The hireling, and he that is not the shepherd, whose own the sheep are not, seeth the wolf coming, and leaveth the sheep, and flieth: and the wolf catcheth, and scattereth the sheep: And the hireling flieth, because he is a hireling: and he hath no care for the sheep (Jn 10:12–13).

Ironically, to achieve His mission of saving His own flock, Christ will become a sheep—the Lamb of God—who allows Himself to be caught by the wolf's grasp for the purpose of liberating and ransoming His sheep. Jesus believes that He is responsible for His flock, and this responsibility is expressed by sacrificing Himself for His flock.

The true shepherd lowers himself to become one with his flock, so that he may know them, and they might know of His faithful love. Often spiritual leaders, spiritual fathers, hire themselves out to labor for the bread that perishes (see Jn 6:27), that is, worldly pursuits, ego, vain ambitions, human respect, carnal lust, and the like, rather than laboring for the "bread of life" (see Jn 6:35), that is, for Jesus and His sheep.

Similar to David the shepherd, Christ the Good Shepherd reveals the source of His confidence and courage: "As the Father knoweth me, and I know the Father: and I lay down my life for my sheep" (Jn 10:15).

Intimate knowledge of God as your Father—and certain knowledge that you are His son, as with Christ—is the very source of strength that inspires the fortitude and charity that is necessary to lay down one's life for others. Divine sonship in Christ affords the son of God the confidence to sacrifice for Christ that others may be inspired to be confident sons of God.

My son, it is knowledge of God that inspires one to love God, and, loving God, you will become like Jesus, who says, "Therefore doth the Father love me: because I lay down my life, that I may take it again" (Jn 10:17), and, in doing as He did, you will become confident that you are loved as He is loved, for it is He who is at work in you.

Lord Jesus, burn the image of your holy face into me
that I may become a revelation of your glory,
that I may proclaim as did the holy Apostle:
"It is no longer I who live, but Christ who lives in me." Amen.

Optional Scripture Readings: John 10:1–14; 1 Kings 17:13–51

FULFILL YOUR SELECTED SPIRITUAL PRACTICES FROM STAGE 4:
SUMMONS TO SACRIFICIAL RESPONSIBILITY.

Day 23

(Lent Week 3: Thursday)

INVOCATION: JESUS, GIVE ME THE GRACE TO
BELIEVE THAT DYING FOR YOU IS LIVING.

LIVING TO DIE

Christ Sets His Gaze on His Destiny

———

"Behold, we go up to Jerusalem, and all things shall be
accomplished." Luke 18:31

Few things in life are as certain as death. If a man lives, that man
will surely die. All plan on living, while few plan on dying. Scarcely
does a man contemplate death, and, more precisely, his own immi-
nent death. Man plans, schemes, and toils without considering that
his day will end abruptly and often without warning. Indeed, a man
saves for tomorrow without considering whether his soul is saved.

"Behold, now you that say: To day or to morrow we will go into
such a city, and there we will spend a year, and will traffic, and make
our gain. Whereas you know not what shall be on the morrow. For
what is your life? It is a vapour which appeareth for a little while,
and afterwards shall vanish away" (Jas 4:13–15).

"Life is given to us that we may learn to die well, and we never think of it. To die well we must live well."[27] Yet, far too often, rather than our love for life not deterring us from death, our love for life deters us from death (see Rev 12:11). We store up wealth for ourselves, amass possessions, build bigger barns to hoard our harvests, and say to ourselves: "Soul, thou hast much goods laid up for many years take thy rest; eat, drink, make good cheer" (Lk 12:19). But God says, "Thou fool, this night do they require thy soul of thee: and whose shall those things be which thou hast provided?" (Lk 12:20).

Jesus, however, is unable to rest until His mission has been consummated: "I have a baptism wherewith I am to be baptized: and how I am straitened until it be accomplished" (Lk 12:50). Jesus expressed that His mission can only be considered fulfilled after He sacrifices Himself for sinners, and, therefore, He sets His face toward Jerusalem, intent on running toward His death:

> Then Jesus took unto him the twelve, and said to them: Behold, we go up to Jerusalem, and all things shall be accomplished which were written by the prophets concerning the Son of man. For he shall be delivered to the Gentiles, and shall be mocked, and scourged, and spit upon: And after they have scourged him, they will put him to death; and the third day he shall rise again. And they understood none of these things. (Lk 18:31–34)

Precisely after Jesus endowed Peter with the keys to His Kingdom, establishing on earth His vicar, Christ set His sights on His departure, His exodus. It is precisely at this moment that Jesus' ministry

27 St. John Vianney, Jill Haak Adels, *Wisdom of the Saints*, 196.

takes a dramatic turn. The disciples, who had believed that the Messiah would liberate Israel from Roman occupation and re-establish the Davidic Kingdom's former glory and splendor, cannot comprehend Christ's words. The Cross as the means of establishing His eternal kingdom is incomprehensible to Jesus' Apostles.

Though surrounded by followers and admired by His Apostles, Christ stands alone. He alone comprehends the weight and burden of His mission. He must bear this weight alone.

Jesus's concept of "kingdom" runs opposite to the world's definition that involves the occupation of lands, ruling of populaces, defined borders, and walled defenses. Such a kingdom is easily targeted. Christ's mission is to liberate man from this concept of national kinship and offer him a greater kingdom—one that cannot be defined by geographical boundaries, nationality, or earthly rulers, and one that cannot be destroyed by simply attacking a certain geographically defined area.

Christ's kingdom cannot be defeated, ultimately, because the Christian is not attached to land or nation, "for lo, the kingdom of God is within [him]" (Lk 17:21). Though the Christian dies, Christ lives on in him, and he lives in Christ for all eternity.

The great paradox of Christ's Gospel is that only by living to die will we truly live. Only by preparing for and embracing a holy death for Christ, will we become alive and holy in Christ.

The worldly man's existence is defined by the fear of losing his life, and, therefore, he lives for the purpose of preserving what he already has. The Christian man is liberated from fear when he desires to spend his life for the One who has imparted life to him. By living in this way, he is no longer bound by fear and, consequently, becomes fully alive.

Indeed, St. John Vianney confirms this paradoxical truth, "I have had crosses in plenty—more than I could carry, almost. I set myself to ask for the love of crosses—then I was happy."[28] Again, "Christ's martyrs feared neither death nor pain. He triumphed in them who lived in them; and they, who lived not for themselves but for Him, found in death the way to life." [29]

My son, to be unconquerable in Christ is to be like the saints, whose love for life did not deter them from death (see Rev 12:11). Therefore, "live as not to fear death. For those who live well in the world, death is not frightening, but sweet and precious."[30]

Lord Jesus, burn the image of your holy face into me
that I may become a revelation of your glory,
that I may proclaim as did the holy Apostle:
"It is no longer I who live, but Christ who lives in me." Amen.

Optional Scripture Readings: Luke 12:15–32; Luke 18: 31–34

FULFILL YOUR SELECTED SPIRITUAL PRACTICES FROM STAGE 4:
SUMMONS TO SACRIFICIAL RESPONSIBILITY.

28   St. John Vianney, Jill Haak Adels, *Wisdom of the Saints*, 63.
29   St. Augustine, *ibid.*
30   St. Rose of Viterbo, *ibid.*

Day 24

(Lent Week 3: Friday)

INVOCATION: JESUS, PROTECT ME FROM AVOIDING
THE SCANDAL OF THE CROSS.

THE TEMPTATION TO AVOID SACRIFICE

Christal Rebukes Peter

"Go behind me, Satan, thou art a scandal
unto me." Matthew 16:23

Precisely after Jesus disclosed to His Apostles His determination to press on toward Jerusalem for the purpose of embracing His Passion and death, Peter took Jesus aside, rebuking Him, "Lord, be it far from thee, this shall not be unto thee. Who turning, said to Peter: Go behind me, Satan, thou art a scandal unto me: because thou savourest not the things that are of God, but the things that are of men" (Mt 16:22–23).

Peter, emboldened by Christ's establishing him as the rock upon which He would build His Church, could not comprehend that the death of their leader could be beneficial. To be judged by the scribes and Pharisees and to be tortured and suffer death at the hands of

Gentile authorities did not appear to be a path to power but rather a curse, a divine disfavor, and an ultimate failure.

Jesus, once again, challenges not only Peter but also all men to open their minds to a new, divine way of thinking: You are setting your mind not on God's ways but man's ways (see Mt 16:23). "For what doth it profit a man, if he gain the whole world, and suffer the loss of his own soul?" (Mt 16:26).

The mind of God reflects His very nature, His essence, which is self-giving love. "God has revealed his innermost secret: God himself is an eternal exchange of love, Father, Son, and Holy Spirit, and he has destined us to share in that exchange" (CCC 221).

Man has been created in God's image for the purpose of reflecting and revealing this divine exchange of love. For his part, man can only discover his true self, true freedom, and true happiness by reflecting, reliving, and revealing God's self-giving love.

In heaven, the divine exchange of love experiences no pain, for there is no selfishness among the Godhead. However, when altruistic love enters a selfish sinful context, such as fallen human existence, giving oneself away to another can become bitterly painful as testified by Christ and His Cross. Yet, it is precisely by sacrificing Himself on full display on the Cross on behalf of sinners that God incarnate reveals definitively God's self-giving love. Yet, the Cross of Christ not only reveals Christ's mission to love but also man's supreme calling, for, as it is said, Christ "fully reveals man to himself and makes his supreme calling clear" (GS, 22).

Satan, the adversary, uses Peter as a bait trap (*scandalon*) in hope of discouraging Jesus from fulfilling His mission of donating Himself for sinful man. The evil one's promise is characterized by a worldly kingdom of power and comfort, devoid of suffering and sacrifice. He instills the alluring lie that sacrifice is not necessary and that suffering must be avoided at all cost. The devil's words, like the fruit which Eve partook in, are outwardly seductive but interiorly saturated with deadly poison.

Satan proposes a prosperity Gospel: Believe and you will receive. The evil one twists God's word to propose that the sign of God's favor and love is personal prosperity, while convincing the Christian that suffering is the curse of God upon man. Yet, it was he, the adversary, the father of lies, who, by seducing Eve, and Adam through Eve, inflicted the consequences of sin upon us, which is suffering.

In fact, to believe that God's love is expressed through prosperity actually tortures many with the haunting doubt that God does not love or care for those who have less or are battered by poverty and suffering. Indeed, suffering is the consequence of evil, and, without being redeemed for a divine purpose, it remains a tragic evil that the Christian is obligated to alleviate. Ironically, it is suffering that inspires the Christian to respond with compassion and to sacrifice himself for the purpose of alleviating another's plight, pain, and anguish.

God's mind is opposed to Satan. God's mission and intent is to give Himself for another that the other may be liberated from bondage to the devil and his selfish ways. Satan's mind, however, is cunning, continually instilling the doubt that self-donation will be too demanding and cost man too much. The evil one attempts to deter the Christian man from embracing heroic sacrifice by multiplying and intensifying doubt and discouragement, hoping that the man will resort to the path of ease and comfort, which is usually the path of disobedience to God's holy will.

Where confusion exists, the devil is present, for confusion is what he instills. Yet, the devil becomes confused by his own confusion.

On one hand, the devil abhors a martyr's death in that it glorifies God. Considering this, he at times hopes that the Christian man will avoid martyrdom. Yet, as his life is prolonged, the Christian man's contagious character thwarts the devils' plans. Consequently, the devil is driven by madness and is determined to destroy the Christian man's life, hoping that he will be forgotten. And, even then, the devil is confounded, for though the man be removed from the earth, the just man's memory cannot be forgotten. Indeed, as the psalmist proclaims, "Surely the righteous will never be shaken; they will be remembered forever" (Ps 112:6, NIV).

The mind of God knows that either by the prolongation of the saint's life, or by his heroic death, God is glorified. For either, by the living testimony of a saint, or by the seed of the martyr's blood, the Church always grows.

Jesus' way is the way of the Cross, and the Cross is His way to freedom and beatitude, and the Cross is man's way to Jesus. Christ and His Cross are inseparable, for it is the Cross that unites Jesus and man, making the two united in God.

"Christ tells us that if we wish to join Him, we shall travel the way He took. It is surely not right that the Son of God should go His way on the path of shame, while the sons of men walk the way of worldly honor."[31]

My son, we, with St. Peter, must shift our understanding from thinking that an earthly utopia of prestige, honor, popularity, and pleasure is the goal. No. The goal is heaven, the kingdom of eternal self-giving love, and the only way to that end is the glorious Cross of Christ.

---

31   St. John of Avila, *ibid.*

Lord Jesus, burn the image of your holy face into me

that I may become a revelation of your glory,

that I may proclaim as did the holy Apostle:

"It is no longer I who live, but Christ who lives in me." Amen.

Optional Scripture Readings: Matthew 16:13–26

FULFILL YOUR SELECTED SPIRITUAL PRACTICES FROM STAGE 4:
SUMMONS TO SACRIFICIAL RESPONSIBILITY.

Day 25

(Lent Week 3: Saturday)

INVOCATION: JESUS, GIVE ME THE GRACE TO
SEEK NOT GLORY FROM MEN.

SACRIFICIAL GLORY

*Tensions Mount Between Christ's Ministry
and the Pharisees*

———————

"I receive glory not from men." John 5:41

Christian freedom is often misunderstood and rarely obtained. Freedom in Christ can never be perceived—as Martin Luther proposed it—as the license to sin while presumptuously relying on God's future mercy. Indeed, God will not be mocked. The reason why freedom in Christ is rarely achieved by the Christian man is because he is enslaved to human opinion and builds his life on its faulty premises.

Indeed, to seek and desire human praise is to be enslaved and bound by the waxing and waning opinions of men. By allowing their identity to be defined by men, men lose their identity as free sons of the Father and are rather slaves to the world, the flesh, and the devil.

While there exist many men who desire to be noticed and renowned among men, there are few men who strive to know God and to be known by God. The respect of men is shifting sand upon which no man should build his house.

As the tensions mount between Christ's public ministry and the legalistic authority of the scribes, Pharisees, and Temple priests, Jesus confronts the religious authorities directly by making an essential distinction that exposes the difference between His ways and the ways of fallen men: "I receive glory not from men" (Jn 5:41).

Saint Thomas Aquinas, commenting on these words of Christ, interprets Jesus' words as meaning: "I do not seek praise from men; for I have not come to be an example of one seeking human glory: 'we did not seek glory from men' (1 Thes 2:6). . . . For I have not come to be glorified by men, but rather to glorify them, since all glory proceeds from Me."[32]

The Jewish leaders used the Law of Moses and religious practices and disciplines for the purpose of glorifying themselves, while Jesus' intention was, and is, to share His glory with men: "And the glory which thou hast given me, I have given to them; that they may be one, as we are also one" (Jn 17:22).

An indication that a man may be enslaved to the apprehension of human glory is his tendency toward jealousy, envy, bitterness, or sadness at another's success or spiritual advancement; party strife; having a spirit of contention; or pursuing vain ambitions. Such envy, ultimately, if left unchecked, leads to the murder of the one who is the cause of our bitterness. Often, this "murder" is in the form of character assassination, which calumniates or detracts from a man's character.

---

32 St. Thomas Aquinas, *Commentary on the Gospel of John*, 315.

Upon the triumphant return of David, Saul, and the Israelite soldiers—after David slew the Philistine giant, and the Israelite army routed the Philistines—the young maidens "sung as they played, and they said: Saul slew his thousands, and David his ten thousands" (1 Sm 18:7). And Saul said, "They have given David ten thousands, and to me they have given but a thousand; what can he have more but the kingdom?" (1 Sm 18:8).

From this point onward, bitter envy polluted and poisoned the heart of Saul, compelling him to seek to kill David (see 1 Sm 18:8; 1 Sm 18:10–16). Saul's enthrallment with vainglory would not allow him to share his glory, nor admit David to have a greater power than himself, because he sought glory only for himself and not for God. Saul is a figure of the religious authorities who opposed Jesus, whose envy of Christ enraged them to the point of plotting his murderous demise.

As Jesus entered Jerusalem and the crowds hailed him as hosanna, "the Pharisees therefore said among themselves: Do you see that we prevail nothing? behold the whole world is gone after him" (Jn 12:19). While the Pharisees lived for obtaining the glory of men, Christ lived to impart to men the glory of God. The two motivations are diametrically opposed to the other.

The glory of God cannot be obtained by an external religious persona but by means of embracing the cruelty and shame of the Cross. If a man seeks the glory of men, men will lead him away from the Cross. If a man embraces the Cross, being freed from the opinions of men, he will obtain the glory of God. "For the word of the cross, to them indeed that perish, is foolishness; but to them that are saved, that is, to us, it is the power of God" (1 Cor 1:18).

The ways of the world seduce men to embrace the effeminate and avoid the Cross. Yet, God warns us, "My thoughts are not your thoughts: nor your ways my ways, saith the Lord" (Is 55:8), "for who hath known the mind of the Lord? Or who hath been his counsellor" (Rom 11:34). Speaking to and of the religious leaders who opposed Him, Jesus said, "You are they who justify yourselves before men, but God knoweth your hearts; for that which is high to men, is an abomination before God" (Lk 16:15).

Our Lord's words should cause us to pause, for when a man lacks belief in God the Father's love, he is lured to seeking that approval from men and becomes conditioned by it, and, doing so, becomes an abomination to God.

But know this, my son, to be a son of God the Father is to walk by faith and not by sight (see 2 Cor 5:7) and to trust in God rather than to trust in princes (see Ps 118:9), for "without faith it is impossible to please God" (Heb 11:6). The faithless seek the praises of men, while the faithful son praises God.

Lord Jesus, burn the image of your holy face into me
that I may become a revelation of your glory,
that I may proclaim as did the holy Apostle:
"It is no longer I who live, but Christ who lives in me." Amen.

Optional Scripture Readings: John 5:32–44; 1 Kings 18:5–12

FULFILL YOUR SELECTED SPIRITUAL PRACTICES FROM STAGE 4:
SUMMONS TO SACRIFICIAL RESPONSIBILITY.

Stage 5

Fourth Week of Lent
SUMMONS TO COMMUNION AND COMPANIONSHIP

During this fifth stage in our Lenten journey, Jesus, knowing the grave
nature of temptation and the weakness of human flesh, pleads with us
to remain with Him, for apart from Him we are hopeless. Jesus reveals
to us that true love will be met with bitter hatred and that His love,
expressed in the Most Holy Sacrament, will become a source of division.
Yet, despite this rejection, Jesus is determined to give man His Body
and Blood, His divine gift of love, for the purpose of providing the few
who will receive Him with a remedy for sin and selfishness. During this
stage, we accompany Jesus in His darkest hours, and, perhaps, loneliest
moments, when all have abandoned Him and His own have betrayed
Him. By means of weekly watches (Holy Hours) with our Lord, frequent
attendance of Holy Mass and reception of Holy Communion (twice
or more a week), and developing a personal litany of thanksgiving,
we apply ourselves to cultivating a profound awe, reverence, and deep
devotion to our Lord in the Most Blessed Sacrament, the Eucharist.
Indeed, we begin to live the thanksgiving sacrifice.

STAGE 5 SPIRITUAL PRACTICES
(SELECT TWO OR THREE)

*The purpose of this stage is to cultivate a true, profound devotion
to our Lord in the Most Blessed Sacrament of the Altar, loving and
worshipping Him in the Eucharist by means of watches, frequent
reception of Holy Communion, and litanies of thanksgiving.*

Attend one extra Holy Mass attendance per week (in addition to Sunday).

Make at least one Holy Hour or add an extra Holy Hour per week.

Develop a personal litany of thanksgiving to be recited while present before the Most Blessed Sacrament.

Day 26

(Lent Week 4: Sunday)

INVOCATION: JESUS, GIVE ME THE GRACE TO REMAIN WITH YOU,
EVEN AMIDST TRIALS AND TERRORS.

REMAINING IN CHRIST

Christ Admonishes His disciples to Remain with Him

———

"Without me you can do nothing." John 15:5

Israel fancied itself as God's Chosen People, for God, through Moses, had proclaimed this much. The chosen vessel of God's glory was often depicted by the prophets and psalmists as God's vine, which He had planted to drive out the Gentile nations, so that it might strike root and be established (see Ps 80:8).

> "The vine had actually become the symbol of the nation Israel. It was
> the emblem on the coins of the Maccabees. One of the glories of the
> Temple was that of a golden vine upon the front of the Holy Place.
> Many a great man had counted it an honor to give gold to mold a new
> bunch of grapes or even a new grape on that vine."[33]

33   Barclay, *Gospel of John*, 201.

Though the vine is associated with the glory of Israel, every scriptural passage that references Israel as the vine is within the context of its degeneracy and failure to produce good fruit (see Is 5:7; Jer 2:21; Hos 10:1; Ps 80:8).[34]

Jesus, while teaching in the Temple, draws a correlation and a distinction between Himself and Israel, and between Himself and the Temple: "I am the vine; you the branches" (Jn 15:5). It is as if Christ is saying to Israel: "Though you believe yourself to be the vine of God, I am the true vine which God has planted. Though you believe that the Temple is the place of worship, I am the ultimate temple of worship." Jesus' words would have been interpreted by the Jews as not only insulting but also blasphemous.

The Jews believed that because they were Israelites by blood, they were the chosen race, superior to other nations, and that the Gentiles—all non-Jews—were not only considered outsiders but filth and refuse, who were destined for wrath.

Our Lord's ministry will soon come under assault. He will be identified as a heretic and a blasphemer, and He will be crushed by this "luxuriant vine," Israel. Considering this, Jesus warns His Apostles in this passage (the fifteenth chapter of John's Gospel) known as "The Vine and the Branches" to "abide" with Him no less than seven times.

The Greek word rendered "abide" is *meno*, which means *to remain*, indicating that, by using this word seven times, Christ is emphatically imploring, if not begging, His disciples not to lose faith in Him and revert to the false premise that simply to be a Jew, a member of Israel, a man of Torah, constitutes whether one is chosen and acceptable to God.

---

34 See Ibid.

Soon, Christ's ministry will come under assault, and His disciples will be scandalized and tempted to remain in the Law rather than remain in Him, to depend on religious affiliation rather than to depend on Christ. Aware of this, Jesus pleads with His disciples to remain in Him, despite how justified Israel will appear.

Jesus is clear, though you will be scandalized, "Abide in me, and I in you. As the branch cannot bear fruit of itself, unless it abide in the vine, so neither can you, unless you abide in me" (Jn 15:4). And again, "I am the vine; you the branches: he that abideth in me, and I in him, the same beareth much fruit: for without me you can do nothing" (Jn 15:5). Jesus's description of Himself as the true vine are applicable and highly relevant for men of all ages, especially the Catholic man who seeks truth in the modern age.

Many a religious man is tempted to make the same mistake that the Jews did who protested, "Abraham is our father." Indeed, earlier, John the Baptist opposed the Jews saying, "And think not to say within yourselves, We have Abraham for our father (Mt 3:9). In other words, it is erroneous to believe that because one is Catholic, and that because he has Peter as his Pope, he is chosen and will be saved.

While the Church's intention is to lead man to Christ by supplying man with the grace Christ offers through the sacraments, often a Catholic man can rely more on the institutional Church than on Christ who established Her. This becomes evident in the person whose focus is primarily on the legalist fulfillment of forms, disciplines, and precepts, while neglecting the true spirit of Christ's precepts.

To be Catholic by name, or to rely on that religious affiliation to procure one's salvation, is not sufficient. Yet, man often places his assurance for salvation on rites, rubrics, disciplines, and traditions rather than on Christ who has allowed these for the purpose of drawing men to Himself. The source of man's salvation in Christ is not the Church per se, for Christ is the source and the Church is the vessel, the reservoir of His saving grace.

When churchmen fail, and certain rites restricted, many are tempted to flee from Christ by leaving His Church, which demonstrates they had more hope and faith in the Church's disciplines and traditions than in He who established them.

Who are we to refuse to remain with Jesus who promises that He is "with you all days, even to the consummation of the world"? (Mt 28:20). While it is true that "all you shall be scandalized" (Mt 26:31), "it is impossible that scandals should not come: but woe to him through whom they come" (Lk 17:1). Yet, when scandals occur, many demonstrate their lack of faith in Christ by either fleeing His Church because of those who cause scandal or neglecting the true doctrine of Christ for the purpose of ignoring the sins of such churchmen. To remain in Christ is to remain obedient to His teachings, to express His unfailing charity, and to receive His life through the sacraments, regardless of rite or minister.

Man, however, wants assurance, safety, security, and certainty, and, therefore, he clings more to a body of believers than to the Head of the body. But, through St. Paul, the Lord convicts us of such false practices: "Now this I say, that every one of you saith: I indeed am of Paul; and I am of Apollo; and I am of Cephas; and I of Christ. Is Christ divided? Was Paul then crucified for you? or were you baptized in the name of Paul?" (1 Cor 1:12–13).

Though a Catholic may affiliate himself exclusively with Paul VI, John XXIII, Pius V, or Pius X, Jesus warns us that we can do nothing apart from Him, for Christ is not divided. "This is not surprising because neither does God do anything without Him, 'without Him was made nothing that was made' (Jn 1:3)."[35]

"With these words [Jesus] instructs the hearts of the humble and silences the mouths of the proud . . . who say that they can do by themselves, without the help of God, the good works of the virtues and of the law. And although they try to maintain our free will, they undermine it."[36]

To glorify God the Father, a son of God must bear much fruit. "In this is my Father glorified; that you bring forth very much fruit, and become my disciples" (Jn 15:8). We are only able to glorify God by bearing fruit. To bear spiritual fruit, one must remain in Christ, and to remain in Christ is to have faith that He is always with us, in our hearts, and in the sacraments, regardless of how corrupt the ministers of the Church become. The Church assures us that grace is always conferred by a sacrament *ex opera operato* (from the work performed) by the virtue of the sacrament itself and not by the virtue of either the minister or the recipient of a sacrament.

Temptations, trials, persecutions, and scandals will arise from outside and from within the Church, and many will be tempted to flee from the true temple and vine, Jesus Christ.

My son, it is not a question of whether the scandals will come, but when and to what severity. Our Lord is emphatic, the true man of God, if he remains in Christ, refusing to flee, will bear much fruit, while those who abandon their posts will be cast into the fire.

35 Ibid., 282.
36 Ibid.

Lord Jesus, burn the image of your holy face into me
that I may become a revelation of your glory,
that I may proclaim as did the holy Apostle:
"It is no longer I who live, but Christ who lives in me." Amen.

Optional Scripture Readings: John 15:1–17; 1 Corinthians 1:10–18

FULFILL YOUR SELECTED SPIRITUAL PRACTICES FROM STAGE 5:
COMMUNION AND COMPANIONSHIP WITH CHRIST.

Day 27

(Lent Week 4: Monday)

INVOCATION: JESUS, EVEN IF I BE HATED,
GIVE ME THE COURAGE TO LOVE.

LOVE THAT INCURS HATRED

Christ Admonishes His Disciples to Radical Charity

"Love one another, as I have loved you." John 15:12

The world's version of virtue is embodied by "getting along," avoiding moral judgements, and proclaiming and living the gospel of "niceness." Peace, kindness, and love are terms that the secular culture has hijacked, disfigured, reinterpreted, and manipulated as an imposition on the Christian man that he might become manageable, even buckle in shame of his moral convictions, and retreat from his steadfast fidelity to his Christian ethical standards.

According to the modern secular cult, to hold fast to one's moral convictions is unkind, uncharitable, and an act of judgment and condemnation of others. For if a man believes truth without imposing it on others, others believe his very presence to be an imposition of his beliefs upon them.

The dictatorship of relativism demands that the Christian man surrender his belief in Christ and adherence to Jesus' commands for the purpose of "keeping the peace." If secularists could identify anything as sinful, it would be the Christian's audacious resolute fidelity to his faith in Christ.

The Gospel of Christ is perceived by contemporary society as a tool of division that causes feuds, strife, and discord, whereas social kindness and peace connote the idea of harmlessness and equality. Yet, when these ideas are wielded by the modern anti-Christian culture, they are used to propagate a lethal tyranny aimed at depriving a man of his ability to express his fidelity to Christ or to call others to fidelity in Christ.

Often, if a man is to establish peace, he must wield the sword of the Gospel; if he is to unite peoples, he must proclaim a truth that often divides; and if he is to love his neighbor, he must hate evil, precisely the evil that binds his neighbor in spiritual death. To love God is to hate evil (see Prov 8:13, Ps 97:10).

With the vision of the Cross and His ignominious death on the horizon, Christ imparted to His disciples, and to us, perhaps His most definitive teaching: "This is my commandment, that you love one another, as I have loved you" (Jn 15:12).

By saying, "This is *my* commandment" (emphasis added), Christ is differentiating His command as having ultimate authority over the Mitzvot (613 legal prescriptions), while also summarizing the Decalogue (the Ten Commandments) into one single divine command.

This raises the question: What love does Jesus speak of? "Greater love than this no man hath, that a man lay down his life for his friends" (Jn 15:13). With this statement, Jesus brings our attention to the fact that He has chosen us to be His friends, and, therefore, He is determined to demonstrate His commitment to this friendship by sacrificing His life to ensure that this friendship endures.

Friendship, by its very nature, is reciprocal. If Christ has chosen us to be His friends, then we must choose Him and His friendship in return. Yet, this friendship with Christ is dependent upon a single principle: that we obey Him. As He says, "You are my friends, if you *do the things that I command you*" (Jn 15:14, emphasis added). And His command is clear: "These things I command you, that you love one another" (Jn 15:17).

Jesus' particular command is that we love as He loves, and to love as He loves demands that we become His friends, and, to be His friends, we are to keep His commands, and His command is that we love one another. To love Christ is to love as Christ loves and to do as He commands. Resolute obedience to Christ's commands, born from a friendship with Him, frustrates the designs of the secularists who realize that they cannot manipulate, control, or bribe the Christian man to surrender His beliefs and moral standards.

Therefore, to love God is to hate evil, and to hate evil is to be hated by the world. For this reason, Jesus warned His disciples and us, "If the world hate you, know ye, that it hath hated me before you" (Jn 15:18). "I have chosen you out of the world, therefore the world hateth you" (Jn 15:19). "If they have persecuted me, they will also persecute you" (Jn 15:20). Love begets love in the heart of one who will receive it. But love can also bring out the worst kind of hatred by those owned and deceived by Satan.

+ JMJ +

Christian love can never be reduced to well-wishing in an effort to "get along," especially with those who maliciously and conspicuously abort human life, attempt to redefine marriage, or propagate transgender ideology wherein a human denies that he is made in God's image and attempts to make himself in his own image, which is human idolatry. Love is truth, and truth, especially when animated by love, draws the vehement hatred of those who oppose it.

To be a friend of another is to "consistently, effectively desire to do good to another."[37] And the greatest good we can do for another is to give them the salvific truth of Christ, which liberates man from being enslaved to evil. Though this love infuriates our enemies, it has the greatest potential to convert them.

The paradoxical Gospel of Jesus is that by loving man you will be hated by men, and, yet, you are to love them nonetheless. By striving for moral goodness, the Christian will be perceived by the world as evil. To be a Christian is to be despised, rejected, unpopular, and hated, even by those whom we love.

My son, friendship has been defined as having the same will. To be Jesus' friend, we are to will what He wills, which is what He commands, and to live His commands is the proof that we love Him, and this love will be contested and hated by the world.

Lord Jesus, burn the image of your holy face into me
that I may become a revelation of your glory,

37   St. Thomas Aquinas, *http://catholicapologetics.info/morality/general/friends.htm.*

that I may proclaim as did the holy Apostle:
"It is no longer I who live, but Christ who lives in me." Amen.

———————

Optional Scripture Readings: John 15:12–19

———————

FULFILL YOUR SELECTED SPIRITUAL PRACTICES FROM STAGE 5:
COMMUNION AND COMPANIONSHIP WITH CHRIST.

Day 28

(Lent Week 4: Tuesday)

INVOCATION: JESUS, GIVE ME THE GRACE TO
BELIEVE IN THE EUCHARIST.

DIVISIVE LOVE

Jesus Gives the Bread of Life Discourse:
The Sacrament of Sacrifice

"Except you eat the flesh of the Son of man . . .
you shall not have life in you." John 6:53

God's ways are not always agreeable to man, nor do they fit
comfortably into his intellectual constructs, and they are
often packaged in ways disagreeable to man's broken nature. Divine
truth often contradicts man's limited understanding and runs
contrary to his interpretation of God's word and testimonies.

In his pursuit of being religious, man often commits the error
of interpreting God's word and the traditions of the Church in a
way that aligns with his lifestyle. He purposefully avoids any unex-
pected theological difficulties that may arise from following Jesus.
He often resists being obedient to God's will when it opposes the

inclinations and preferences that he has become dependent on. This is a very common plight among men of sincerity, who in pursuit of truth eventually encounter challenging difficulties when attempting to embrace Christ's teachings. Ultimately, the believer is faced with either altering his view, which could have tremendous ramifications on the way he lives, demanding severe sacrifices, or avoiding those difficult teachings of the Gospel and remaining on his predetermined course.

Man toggles between the continual tension of conforming himself to Jesus and His teachings and conforming Jesus and His teachings to himself. Christ, however, is not interested in coercing man to obey His precepts in a spirit of slavish fear but rather desires that we become faithful sons who live in holy abandon to His divine will.

To increase our faith and our capacity for His presence living within us, He often calls us to press beyond our calculated certainty that offers us a sense of spiritual security. Often, our Lord's truth, so contradictory to our preferences and affections, is a veiled invitation to rely solely on Him and to act in faith, especially when our intellectual, emotional, and physical senses fail to comprehend His divine logic.

Perhaps, no other teaching exemplifies this perplexing dynamic as evidently as our Lord's "Bread of Life Discourse" (see Jn 6:22–59), wherein seven times, in seven different phrases, Jesus confirms that He is the bread of life, that this "bread" *is* His flesh, and that one *must* eat His flesh and drink His blood to have His life within him.

To reinforce the meaning of these cryptic phrases, Jesus uses a very vivid Greek word (*trōgōn*), rendered eat in the vernacular (see Jn 6:56), which actually means to gnaw, munch, or crunch.

Jesus pressed His Jewish listeners beyond their intellectual reasoning, calling them to radical faith in Him. Not only is the idea of eating another human being's flesh contrary to human custom, but such an idea directly violated the Jewish Law, which condemned the drinking of blood (see Lv 17:14; Dt 12:23). Additionally, the act of cannibalism was understood by the Jews as a consequence of God's judgment for sin (see Lv 26:27–30; Jer 19:7–10; Dt 28:52–57; 2 Kgs 6:26–29).

Yet, Christ knows that "without faith it is impossible to please God" (Heb 11:6), and, therefore, with the intent to save man's soul, He offers him the opportunity to move beyond his own limited understanding and rely on Him alone.

Once again, Jesus highlights the truth that the Law cannot save man, but Christ alone saves. To save a few, Jesus spoke a truth that lost many. After Jesus' followers heard His command regarding the eating of His flesh, they no longer went about with Him and returned to their former way of life (see Jn 6:67).

Even today, among Christians, the Eucharist remains the central object of debate and division and provides a decision point for conversion. Protestants either ignore the Bread of Life discourse systematically or interpret Christ's words as hyperbolic and, therefore, figurative and symbolic.

To interpret our Lord's words as symbolic is impossible, for He re-stated Himself on this matter seven times, seven being the perfect number, symbolic of a covenantal oath, as if to say, "I am swearing an oath to you." This is evident in His words during the Last Supper, which conferred the Eucharistic species: This is the blood of the new and everlasting covenant (see Luke 22:20). When those who could not bear this difficult teaching left our Lord, He did *not* clarify that He was speaking figuratively; rather, He pressed on with only a limited following.

Some Catholics refrain from receiving the Eucharist when it is offered in certain liturgical rites that are not preferential or deemed deficient or circumspect, believing that Christ is either not present, or present in a reduced or limited way. Even today, Jesus' gift of His flesh and blood is often rejected by man because of his limited appreciation for the miraculous nature of the Eucharist.

The Eucharist is the sign of divine sonship, for it is Christ's faith in us that believes His words to be true: We must eat His flesh and drink His blood, or we have no life within us (see Jn 6:53). To trust in this miraculous gift is the sign as to whether one is truly a son of God the Father, for "he that eateth my flesh, and drinketh my blood, abideth in me, and I in him (Jn 6:56).

For man to abide forever in Christ, Christ must abide in man. God became man and, as the God-man, He supplies His divinized flesh to spiritually empower man's corrupt flesh, that he may be empowered to sacrifice his body, precisely because of the sacrificial and resurrected body of Christ that he partakes in. Indeed, Jesus gives us His sacrificed, living flesh that we may become a living sacrifice (see Rom 12:1). Jesus provides the flesh that conquered death that He, in us, may conquer death. One who partakes in the Eucharist is no cannibal, for a cannibal takes and consumes a dead victim, whereas Jesus gives man His living, resurrected, glorified, yet sacrificed body.

There exist those who reject this miraculous gift of Christ's Eucharist due to non-belief, but there are also those who do so by idolizing the context in which it is freely given. The Mass itself is not the Eucharist per se but rather the context in which Christ gives

Himself to us. The two, though intrinsically integrated, are not the same, for the Mass is not the sacrament of the altar per se.

To reject Christ's sacrificial offering in the Eucharist because one does not prefer the rite or the minister of the rite in which Christ offers Himself is to prefer the rite over the reason for the rite, the priest over the Great High Priest and victim, the context of the offering over the offering itself. Such a man prefers the law over the spirit of the law.

Jesus harshly condemned this type of piety: "Woe to you blind guides, that say . . . whosoever shall swear by the altar, it is nothing; but whosoever shall swear by the gift that is upon it, is a debtor. Ye blind: for whether is greater, the gift, or the altar that sanctifieth the gift?" (Mt 23:16, 18–19). In other words, which is greater, that which sanctifies or the context in which the sanctification is given; the Holy Sacrament of the Eucharist or the rubrics and rites that contextualize the sacrifice?

The context that surrounds the Most Holy Sacrifice of the Mass has most assuredly changed over the centuries. Though the rite may change, Christ's Eucharist is unchangeable, for "Jesus Christ is the same yesterday and today and forever" (Heb 13:8, NIV). And again, "for by one oblation he hath perfected for ever them that are sanctified" (Heb 10:14), meaning that the sacrifice of Jesus Christ that commenced on Calvary is the same sacrifice that every believer partakes in at *every* Holy Mass.

During the infancy of the early Church, the Mass was called *eucharistia* (thanksgiving), indicating that even the name of the context has changed. Therefore, "in all things give thanks (*eucharisteite*); for this is the will of God in Christ Jesus" (1 Thes 5:18), that is, in all valid and approved liturgical contexts, "for Christ our pasch is sacrificed" (1 Cor 5:7), and, as Christ tells us, "He that eateth my flesh, and drinketh my blood, abideth in me, and I in him" (Jn 6:56).

My son, though the context of the divine gift may change, the gift of Christ's divine love never alters, for the gift of God is irrevocable (see Rom 11:29). Therefore, remain always with Christ, that Christ may always remain in you.

Lord Jesus, burn the image of your holy face into me
that I may become a revelation of your glory,
that I may proclaim as did the holy Apostle:
"It is no longer I who live, but Christ who lives in me." Amen.

Optional Scripture Readings: John 6:32–55; Matthew 23:1–36

FULFILL YOUR SELECTED SPIRITUAL PRACTICES FROM STAGE 5:
COMMUNION AND COMPANIONSHIP WITH CHRIST.

Day 29

(Lent Week 4: Wednesday)

Invocation: Jesus, give me the divine remedy for sin.

The Divine Remedy for Sin

The Last Supper: Jesus Gives His Flesh to Eat

"Take ye, and eat. . . . This is my body" . . .
"which is given for you." Matthew 26:26; Luke 22:19

Catholicism has been portrayed incorrectly as a religion that imposes oppressive rules and regulations that induce guilt and condemnation on its members. Opponents to Catholicism attempt to dismiss it by dismissing the law altogether, deeming it completely unnecessary.

To dismiss the law is to dismiss the hope of receiving God's mercy. For if a man is to become aware of his need for God's mercy and forgiveness, it is imperative that he be convinced of his sin and, therefore, comprehend the consequence of condemnation that is a direct result of his sin. Mercy cannot be received by one who believes that he has no need of it. Therefore, the law is necessary.

No man can save his own soul or procure his own salvation by a strict adherence to the either the old Law (Torah) or the "New Law," for the ransom of man's soul is beyond him (see Ps 49:8), and no man is justified by the works of the Law (see Rom 3:20).

The purpose of the law is to reveal to man that he is unable to save himself, "for if there had been a law given which could give life, verily justice should have been by the law" (Gal 3:21). Therefore, the law exists that man may be convicted by it and, therefore, in humility appeal to God for His mercy.

Far from being a cult of religious prescriptions, Catholicism is a cult of mercy, "for God sent not his Son into the world, to judge the world, but that the world may be saved by him" (Jn 3:17). And, as Christ Himself testifies, "I came not to call the just, but sinners to penance" (Lk 5:32), "for the Son of man is come to seek and to save that which was lost" (Lk 19:10) "not . . . to be ministered unto, but to minister, and to give his life a redemption for many" (Mk 10:45).

Though Jesus has won for man justification in the sight of God, sin continues to vex man, and the residue of its plague lingers and secretly accuses him. So disheartening is the reality of one's own sin that many a preacher avoids the use of the word sin and replaces it with "struggles," "weaknesses," "shortcomings," and "failings." Indeed, man resents and resists the ugly reality of his own sins, and those who condemn sin.

If we are to embrace the goodness of Christ, it is imperative that we confront the reality and consequences of our sins. Sin is a violation against God and His commands; it is "a word, deed, or desire in opposition to the eternal law,"[38] which is love of God and love of neighbor (see Mt 22:36–40). Sin separates man from God and is that which constitutes the state of separation from God.

38 St. Augustine, *Contra Faustum*, 22, 27, PL 44, 418.

The Greek word rendered sin is *hamartia*, which literally means to miss the mark as in an archery competition. Sin, missing the mark, is a failure to win, to receive the prize, which is communion with God and entering into heavenly beatitude. A man sins when he misses the mark of living for and loving like God.

Sin occurs when something good is divorced from its good purpose yet remains connected to the good. For example, water is good and has been created for the good purpose of hydrating human beings. However, if a human being ingests water through his nose, transferring it into his lungs, he runs the risk of dying from suffocation.

Rest is good. The good purpose of rest is to regenerate man's mind and body that he may continue to complete his work with efficiency and excellence. Yet, resting excessively for the purpose of avoiding work becomes sloth, and, in this case, rest is divorced from its intended purpose.

Sexual intercourse is pleasurable, and its good purpose is procreation, unification of spouses, and the redemption of man from selfishness. Yet, fornication, infidelity, and pornography are evil acts, for they are divorced from the intended purpose of human sexuality.

Though the good of water, rest, and sexual intercourse may be abused and separated from their intended good purpose, they cannot be separated from their essential good. For example, though sexual desire is misused, the pleasure of a disordered sexual act remains.

This is precisely why sin is seductive: the goodness of the creature (water, rest, conjugal love) is not removed when it is used for a sinful purpose.

Nevertheless, "sin deprives us of communion with God and therefore makes us incapable of eternal life" (CCC 1472). "Mortal sin destroys charity (friendship with God) in the heart," for it prefers "an inferior good to him" (CCC 1855). Hence, to be a friend of Jesus is to keep His commands, not transgress them.

Sin, therefore, is a void in man's soul. It is a removal of God's love that is replaced with a disordered love for created things; thus, "the wages of sin is death" (Rom 6:23).

We discover the foundational reason for acting sinfully in the original sin of our first parents, who, desiring to be like God, did not believe that God desired to share His glory with them, and, therefore, they allowed their trust in their Creator to die in their hearts (see CCC 397).

Sin, then, is always a distrust of God and His fatherly generosity. When a man distrusts the benevolence of God, he conditions himself to grasp for that which he thinks God has forbidden. This is one of the reasons why Jesus, on the eve preceding His death, said to His disciples, "With desire I have desired to eat this pasch with you, before I suffer" (Lk 22:15). Jesus, from all eternity, desired to give unto man His flesh to eat.

During this Passover rite, "Jesus took bread, and blessed, and broke: and gave to his disciples, and said: Take ye, and eat. This is my body" (Mt 26:26), "which is given for you" (Lk 22:19). "And taking the chalice, he gave thanks, and gave to them, saying: Drink ye all of this. For this is my blood of the new testament, which shall be shed for many unto remission of sins" (Mt 26:27–28); "Do this for a commemoration of me" (Lk 22:19).

The only occasion in the New Testament that the New Covenant is mentioned is by Christ Himself in the context of giving to the faithful the Most Holy Eucharist. A covenant differs from a contract in that is it not a mere exchange of goods but, much like a marriage, is a pledge of persons who give themselves unto the other through an oath.

Jesus, by giving the Most Holy Eucharist, is pledging Himself to man that man may become capable of pledging himself to God. Jesus' plea to "do this for a commemoration of me" is His summons for man to participate (*koinónia*) in the Eucharistic sacrifice. Indeed, the Eucharist is a covenantal exchange of persons, a remembrance that Jesus has given His Body and Blood as an eternal testimony, a perpetual promise, that regardless of the horror and filth of one's sin, if the sinner but turn to Christ and repent, He will never cast him out, for as He promises, "And him that cometh to me, I will not cast out" (Jn 6:37). In the moment of receiving Holy Communion, not only does Christ give Himself to repentant man, but man gives himself to God in Christ. This is man's participation (*koinónia*) in the covenant.

My son, Jesus' Body and Blood affords your body the power to do what God the Son accomplished with His body: He trusted God so completely that He sacrificed His flesh for the sake of sinners. The Eucharist instills in man the trust that is necessary to overcome the distrust caused by sin.

Lord Jesus, burn the image of your holy face into me
that I may become a revelation of your glory,
that I may proclaim as did the holy Apostle:
"It is no longer I who live, but Christ who lives in me." Amen.

———

Optional Scripture Readings: Matthew 26:26–28;
Luke 22:15–22; 1 Corinthians 11:23–30

———

FULFILL YOUR SELECTED SPIRITUAL PRACTICES FROM STAGE 5:
COMMUNION AND COMPANIONSHIP WITH CHRIST.

Day 30

(Lent Week 4: Thursday)

INVOCATION: JESUS, GIVE ME THE GRACE TO FOLLOW
YOU INTO YOUR AGONY.

SACRIFICIAL PERSEVERANCE

Jesus' Agony in Gethsemane

"Abba, Father . . . remove this chalice from me." Mark 14:36

Trust is the fundamental element of any true and enduring relationship. A relationship lacking trust will lack love, and, without love, it becomes bereft of real sacrifice, and, without sacrifice, a true communion of persons cannot be forged.

Sacrifice for another is proof of love for the other. Love compels one to sacrifice, and sacrifice demonstrates love compellingly. Trust is the catalyst, which empowers a man to give himself, with confidence, in self-donation to another and for the other, hoping that the gift of self will be received.

Jesus' entire mission, at its very core, was and is to forge an enduring bond of trust between God the Father and His incredulous children. Jesus came to reveal God as Father, as His Father, and as our Father.

+ JMJ +

Underscoring this purpose, when asked by His disciples to teach them how to pray, Jesus responded, "Thus therefore shall you pray: Our Father . . . " (Mt 6:9). It is interesting to note that in Aramaic, the language that Jesus spoke, as well as in the Greek and Latin translations, the emphasis is on the word "Father," which occurs first (e.g., *Pater Noster*) and is modified by the word "our," thus signifying that Jesus would like us to begin our prayer by focusing on *Abba, Pater, Father*.

This "first word" is an endearing term that fosters intimacy and trust. It is as if one is saying, "God, you are my Father, and I your son."

Fear, however, particularly of God and His omnipotence, righteousness, and just judgement, and, at times, His apparent lack of intervention, bites at and debilitates our willingness to trust Him with abandon. Fear is nearly always rooted in the potential loss of something that we hold dear or love, or have become attached to. Though it is difficult for a son of God to admit, daily he is tempted to believe that God's intent is to take what he has, to cause him suffering, and to inflict punishment and pain.

A most striking example of this tension to trust in the face of apparent divine adversity is expressed in the account of the patriarch Abraham being commanded by God to sacrifice his son, his only son, whom he loved (see Gen 22:2). It seems incomprehensible that God, after finally answering Abraham's prayer for a son from his own loins, commands him to sacrifice that son. Indeed, Abraham and Sarah gave their son the name Isaac, which means laughter—their elated response to being able to conceive a child at an impossibly old age. This joy, however, was turned into mourning with God's command to sacrifice Isaac.

Yet, Abraham, obedient unto the Lord, sets himself to the task of sacrificing Isaac on Mount Moriah. As the two climbed toward the place of sacrifice, Isaac said, "My father" (Gen 22:7), to which Abraham answered, "Here am I, my son" (Gen 22:7, ASV). Isaac asks, "Behold, the fire and the wood. But where is the lamb for a burnt-offering?" (Gen 22:7, ASV). "Abraham answered, 'God himself will provide the lamb'" (Gen 22:8, NIV).

Obedient unto the divine command, Abraham bound Isaac, which implies that the act was against Isaac's free will (see Gen 22:9). Yet, God, through the angel, steadied the hand of Abraham, restraining him from fulfilling the command: "Lay not thy hand upon the boy, neither do thou any thing to him: now I know that thou fearest God, and hast not spared thy only begotten son for my sake" (Gen 22:12).

By means of this terrifying account, God teaches His children that a father is to never sacrifice the life of his son, but rather only a willing Son can offer himself in sacrifice to his Father; second, God Himself will provide the sacrificial Lamb; third, that the sacrifice of the Lamb will be His only begotten Son; and fourth, God will not force His Son to sacrifice Himself, but rather His Son will choose to offer Himself freely. Christ indicates this when He says, "No man taketh [my life] from me: but I lay it down of myself" (Jn 10:18) (which includes God the Father), and again, "He was offered because it was his own will" (Is 53:7).

Jesus' mission was to demonstrate that to be a son of God is to trust God the Father completely, even unto death. By doing so, He proved that faithful sonship is ultimately rewarded with victory over the grave and a sharing in the eternal glory of God.

Yet, the life of Christ demonstrates the intense and tenacious character of this battle to trust God the Father and His divine will.

The night prior to Jesus' Crucifixion, shortly after He instituted the Most Holy Eucharist, Jesus led His disciples to the Garden of Gethsemane. "And he was withdrawn away from them a stone's cast; and kneeling down, he prayed" (Lk 22:41), "Abba, Father, all things are possible to thee: remove this chalice from me; but not what I will, but what thou wilt" (Mk 14:36).

Notice that the first word of Christ, in His moment of intense desperation, is "Abba." Christ, the typological fulfillment of Isaac, cries out as did Isaac, "Father!" As Isaac carried the wood for the sacrifice up Mount Moriah, so Christ will carry the Cross up Mount Calvary; but, what Isaac could not do by his own free will, Christ will do freely; and what Abraham was intent to do against Isaac's will, God the Father will not do against Jesus' free will.

Jesus not only taught us by word but by His actions to pray, "Abba, Father." *Abba* is the Aramaic word for father, yet distinct from the Greek word *Pater*. Abba is a term that demonstrates filial tenderness and intimacy as well as trust and obedience.

Jesus calling God *Abba*, in this most dire moment of His agony, communicates total abandonment, intimate filial tenderness, and an unreserved act of total obedience. With this prayer, during His hour of agony, Christ teaches us that man's greatest battle is to maintain his divine sonship, especially in the face of the most severe trials.

The marked difference between the slave and the son of God is that the son, even amidst the most severe tests and temptations, can call God his *Abba* and believe that with Him "all things are possible" (Mk 14:36).

Ironically, the word *agony*, which Christ underwent, comes from the Greek root word *ago*, which means to be guided or led away.

Often, God our Father, leads us by means of agonies, situations of great fear, anxiety, and terror, so that, persevering through it all, we may become triumphant and trusting sons of God, in God the Son.

My son, your life will be comprised of countless trials and acute tests that offer you the opportunity to become a true and trusting son of the Father, who in the face of potential loss has the courage and audacity to believe that God is *Abba, Pater.*

Lord Jesus, burn the image of your holy face into me
that I may become a revelation of your glory,
that I may proclaim as did the holy Apostle:
"It is no longer I who live, but Christ who lives in me." Amen.

Optional Scripture Readings: Luke 22:39–46;
Mark 14:32–42; Genesis 22:1–14

FULFILL YOUR SELECTED SPIRITUAL PRACTICES FROM STAGE 5:
COMMUNION AND COMPANIONSHIP WITH CHRIST.

Day 31

(Lent Week 4: Friday)

INVOCATION: JESUS, GIVE ME THE GRACE TO NEVER ABANDON YOU.

WEAKNESS OF THE FLESH

Jesus Is Abandoned in His Agony

———

"Could you not watch one hour with me?" Matthew 26:40

R arely does man reflect on Jesus' radical, perpetual self-denial. Often Christians misinterpret the Word becoming flesh as a temporal reality—that after Christ completed His earthly pilgrimage and ascended into heaven, as one removes a robe or a shirt, He removed the garment of His humanity forever, returning to His former status of being solely divine.

Christ's love for mankind, however, is permanent, as expressed by the fact that "he is able also to save for ever them that come to God by him; always living to make intercession for us" (Heb 7:25). Jesus, in His resurrected humanity, presents Himself on behalf of the human race to His Father, forever. Consequently, Christ, though glorified in heaven, retains a human heart, a heart that suffers in His body of believers, the poor, the outcast, the lonely, and the suffering, as confirmed by his plea to Saul, who was persecuting the early Christian Church, "Saul, Saul, why persecutest thou me?" (Acts 9:4).

Jesus' ability to suffer in the depth of His soul is highlighted powerfully during His agony in the garden. Jesus, with full knowledge of the evil that would be unleashed upon Him over the course of the next day, prayed, "Abba, Father, all things are possible to thee: remove this chalice from me; but not what I will, but what thou wilt" (Mk 14:36). "And he cometh to his disciples, and findeth them asleep, and he saith to Peter: What? Could you not watch one hour with me?" (Mt 26:40). His closest Apostles, in their sleep of sorrow, neglected the Lord the company that He desired.

In this plea, Jesus reveals two things of importance: first, He desires the consolation of human friendship; second, He desires that we "watch" for the purpose of overcoming and conquering temptation. This passage also reveals that Jesus has provided a single way for us to accomplish both of these divine desires: watch with Him.

Friendship is to desire effectively and consistently the good of another.[39] If we are friends with Christ, we desire His good—what He wills. And "it is not good for man to be alone" (Gen 2:18). Notice that Jesus in the garden was alone: His sleeping Apostles neglected Him, and, ultimately, after His arrest, they fled. Yet, it is not good that even the God-man be alone.

But He is alone. Jesus, who has extended His Real Presence in a most hidden, silent, little way in the Most Holy Eucharist, more often than not, watches alone, waiting for someone to be with Him, that He may be with that someone.

Christ promises, "Behold I am with you all days, even to the

39　See St. Thomas Aquinas, *http://catholicapologetics.info/morality/general/friends.htm.*

consummation of the world" (Mt 28:20). But are we with Him? Do we watch "for even one hour" with Him? Imprisoned in tabernacles throughout the world, Jesus waits for those whom He loves to console His human heart, that, by consoling His heart, He may console theirs. Though Christ's Eucharistic presence is abused, neglected, and flippantly consumed, often only temporarily considered after reception but soon forgotten, His greatest sadness, perhaps, is caused by those who fall into temptation and are devoured by the devil.

This is one reason why He commands us to pray, "Lead us not into temptation" (Mt 6:13); "Watch ye, and pray that ye enter not into temptation. The spirit indeed is willing, but the flesh weak" (Mt 26:41); therefore, "be sober and watch: because your adversary the devil, as a roaring lion, goeth about seeking whom he may devour" (1 Pt 5:8). Because of this, Jesus commands, "And what I say to you, I say to all: Watch" (Mk 13:37). Jesus' remedy to overcome temptation is to be alert with Him and to remain with Him, awake and watching one hour in His holy Eucharistic presence.

Watching with Christ is imperative and key to conquering the devil and to not abandoning Jesus. Peter and the Apostles, rather than heeding the command to watch, were overcome with a deep sleep. Upon awakening, they discovered the horrific and startling reality that Judas had betrayed Christ. Caught off guard, seized with panic, they all abandoned their friend, rabbi, and Lord.

Our Lord promises that if we remain in Him, He will remain in and with us (see Jn 15:4). To assist us with remaining with Him, He offers us a most fitting way to remain and watch one hour with Him in the context of Eucharistic Adoration. By frequent visits with our Lord in the Most Blessed Sacrament of the Altar, we enter into the presence of God, whose presence enters into us, endowing us with the strength to overcome temptation.

Indeed, as King David expresses, "O God, my God, to thee do I *watch* at the break of day. For thee my soul hath thirsted; for thee my flesh, O how many ways! In a desert land, and where there is no way, and no water: so in the *sanctuary* have *I come before thee*, to see thy power and glory" (Ps 63:1-2, emphasis added).

Those who rise early in the morning and visit our Lord, watching and being present before His presence in the sanctuary where He resides in the tabernacle, will console Jesus' Sacred Heart and begin to experience God's power and glory in their own lives.

My son, it is the little, silent, hidden power of the Eucharist that conquers the temptation to deem our worth from the world and its maxims. Indeed, the paradox of greatness is that by looking upon the little, silent, hidden Christ in the Eucharist, our littleness may express His greatness, our silence may speak profoundly of His grace, and our hiddenness in Him may reveal His glory.

Lord Jesus, burn the image of your holy face into me
that I may become a revelation of your glory,
that I may proclaim as did the holy Apostle:
"It is no longer I who live, but Christ who lives in me." Amen.

Optional Scripture Readings: Matthew 26:36–46; Psalms 62; John 15:1–11

FULFILL YOUR SELECTED SPIRITUAL PRACTICES FROM STAGE 5:
COMMUNION AND COMPANIONSHIP WITH CHRIST.

Day 32

(Lent Week 4: Saturday)

INVOCATION: JESUS, GIVE ME THE STRENGTH TO ENDURE TRIALS
THAT I MAY ANOINT OTHERS WITH YOUR LOVE.

THE OIL PRESS OF CHARITY

Jesus Is Betrayed by Judas

"Dost thou betray the Son of man with a kiss?" Luke 22:48

T he eve preceding His Crucifixion, Jesus withdrew into the shadows of the Garden of Gethsemane, imploring His disciples to watch and pray with Him.

The garden was Jesus' and His disciple's private place of respite (see Jn 18:2), a safe refuge from the crowds. A figure of the Garden of Eden, a paradise in which God placed Adam, Gethsemane was a place of peace for the New Adam and His inner circle.

It is highly appropriate and significant that this garden is the context for Jesus' ultimate confrontation with evil. Adam, the original man, whom God granted dominion over the garden, was given the commands to till and keep the garden. The word rendered till, *abad* in Hebrew, means to cherish, and the word rendered keep, *shamar* in Hebrew, means to protect. The word garden was often used in Hebrew literature as a symbol of woman, her interiority, her dignity, and her fruitfulness. For example, "My sister, my spouse, is a garden enclosed, a garden enclosed, a fountain sealed up" (Song 4:12). From these insights, we can deduce that God warned Adam that evil existed, and that it was Adam's noble duty to ensure that this evil did not penetrate his dominion of the garden.

Yet, when Adam is confronted by the "evil serpent," the devil, he faulted at his post and neglected to stand in the breach between the devil and his wife, Eve. Adam allowed the serpent to slither his way, not only into Eden, but into the garden of Eve's soul, penetrating her with sin, and, thus, death was transmitted through her to all her children.

Though the garden, symbolic of woman, can be a type of paradise and delight for the man, as the name Eden signifies, it is also the context of the spiritual battle. The word rendered *Gethsemane* means "oil press." The Garden of Gethsemane was used as an oil press. During a process called treading, a stone would crush the olive, and the oil of the olive was collected.

From these figures, we can conclude, allegorically, that if a man holds fast to his sacrificial responsibility to cherish and protect his bride, he will, indeed, be "treaded" that the oil of charity be extracted from him and poured lavishly on his wife and children. This patriarchal sacrifice is the key to the conversion of families in Christ. Indeed, society goes by way of the family, and the family goes by way of the father.

As Judas, the cohort of Temple guards, and a vast multitude with swords and clubs entered the garden, Jesus "went forth, and said to them: Whom seek ye?" (Jn 18:4). Unlike the original Adam, the

New Adam, Jesus Christ, courageously stepped into the breach, as demonstrated by the phrase He "went forth," protecting (*shamar*) His bride, the nascent Church, comprised of His Apostles, and demanding that the crowds "let these go there way" (Jn 18:8).

It is here in the "oil press" that the process of Christ's "treading" commences, as demonstrated by His sweating drops of blood. Because of His willingness to be "crushed" (see Is 53:10), His oil of charity anoints each of us, converting our souls.

This process of Jesus' "treading" was triggered by Judas Iscariot's treacherous betrayal of Christ. "And forthwith coming to Jesus, [Judas] said: Hail, Rabbi. And he kissed him" (Mt 26:49). To which Jesus responded, "Judas, dost thou betray the Son of man with a kiss?" (Lk 22:48).

"But there is something dreadful here. When Judas says, 'Whom I shall kiss, that is he,' he uses the word [Greek] *philein*, which is the ordinary word [for kiss]. But when it is said that he came forward and kissed Jesus, the word is *kataphilein*. The kata is intensive and suggests that the kiss was prolonged in order to give a clear sign."[40] The word *kataphileson,* the actual Greek word describing Judas' kiss, means "to kiss frequently or repeatedly."

Judas' betrayal serves as a severe warning to the Bride of Christ, the members of His Church, who receive His Most Sacred Body and Blood repeatedly, kissing Him with their mouths, yet without repenting with their hearts. Indeed, to receive the Eucharist—the sign of the spousal union between the eternal bridegroom and the bride, the Church—without repenting of one's evil actions, or while in the state of mortal sin, is kissing the Lord: the ultimate sign of betrayal.

---

40 Barclay, *Gospel of Mark*, 403.

Saint Paul, speaking on the matter of reception of our Lord's sacred body, sternly warns, "Therefore whosoever shall eat this bread, or drink the chalice of the Lord unworthily, shall be guilty of the body and of the blood of the Lord" (1 Cor 11:27), "for he that eateth and drinketh unworthily, eateth and drinketh judgment to himself, not discerning the body of the Lord" (1 Cor 11:29). Notice that not only is it a grave sin to receive the Eucharist unworthily but also to receive the Bread of Life without discerning—that is believing—it to be the body and blood of our Lord Jesus.

The heinous sin of Judas was that, though he ceased to believe in Christ, he neglected to leave Him. Though, in his heart, Judas ceased being a follower of Jesus, he nevertheless appeared as one, which made him an inside traitor. This is evident in the account of Jesus' Bread of Life discourse, wherein, after Jesus said that one must eat His flesh and drink His blood, "many of his disciples went back; and walked no more with him" (Jn 6:66). Yet, Judas remained. Because of this, "Jesus answered them: Have not I chosen you twelve; and one of you is a devil? Now he meant Judas Iscariot, the son of Simon: for this same was about to betray him, whereas he was one of the twelve" (Jn 6:70–71).

There are many who, while rejecting Christ and His Church's teachings, remain in the Church, or, not believing in the "true presence," continue to receive Christ's Body and Blood. They are traitors who heap judgment upon themselves. Fearful to leave the flock and lose face, they have already lost Christ and the ability to seek His face.

Judas "was a thief, and as he kept the money box, he used to steal from what was put into it" (Jn 12:6, NASB). Many approach Jesus in the manner that Judas did, hoping to receive from Christ without surrendering themselves to Him. When Christ does not give them the worldly favors that they desire, they betray Him with an outward demonstration of devotion, but inwardly they resent Him.

My son, if you are to "kiss" the Son of God properly, it is imperative that you first repent and then receive so that you may be strengthened to endure the necessary process of treading, so that others may receive Christ's oil of charity from you.

Lord Jesus, burn the image of your holy face into me
that I may become a revelation of your glory,
that I may proclaim as did the holy Apostle:
"It is no longer I who live, but Christ who lives in me." Amen.

Optional Scripture Readings: Genesis 2:15–17; Luke 22:46–51;

John 18:1–9; John 6:66–71; 1 Corinthians 11:23–30

FULFILL YOUR SELECTED SPIRITUAL PRACTICES FROM STAGE 5:
COMMUNION AND COMPANIONSHIP WITH CHRIST.

Extra Reflection

(Lent Week 4)

REAL REPENTANCE

Peter Denies Christ

"But I have prayed for thee." Luke 22:32

God does not define a Christian by sin, but rather by how he responds to sin. "Sin is shameful only when we commit it, but being converted into confession and penance, it becomes honorable and wholesome—contrition and confession, being so beautiful . . . as to efface its deformity and purify its stench."[41]

Repentance of one's sins becomes the means that leads one to receive the grace of purification of one's sins. "What then? shall we sin, because we are not under the law, but under grace? God forbid?" (Rom 6:15).

Though repentance from sin makes available the reception of God's grace, forgiveness, and mercy, this does not give us license to sin; rather, we are to fight to the death in our efforts to avoid sin and

---

41 St. Francis de Sales, *Introduction to A Devout Life* (New York: Frederick Pustet & Co., 1900.

demonstrate that we are faithful friends of Jesus. As Dominic Savio said, "Death, but not sin!"[42]

Considering this, the truth is that you will sin. But how you respond after that shameful moment has the potential to determine your life's trajectory and, indeed, your eternal destiny.

Two of the most notable examples of man's response to sin is Judas Iscariot and Peter, the Prince of the Apostles. Both Judas and Peter sinned gravely against Jesus and their intimate confidence with Him.

Upon realizing that Jesus' kingdom would not be founded upon and established by worldly power, Judas Iscariot appealed to the priestly class and Pharisees in hopes of obtaining some type of lucrative benefit for knowing Jesus: "What will you give me, and I deliver [Jesus] unto you?" (Mt 26:15).

Though we may envision ourselves as different than Judas, often our intentions are marked by his motivations. Often, man's relationship with Jesus is founded upon *quid pro quo*: "What will you give me?" The misguided Christian looks at his faith as a means to extract the most from God's divine benevolence while exercising the least amount of personal investment and self-giving. His subconscious motto is: "What can God give me?"

It is a common practice among worldly Christians to use faith, religion, and our relationship with God as a means to obtain a hoped-for temporal end. To determine whether we are guilty of this dynamic, we may ask ourselves: What does my prayer consist of—petitions or praise, grumbling or thanksgiving, Lord give me this or that, or Lord give me you?

---

42 St. Dominic Savio, Jill Haak Adels, *Wisdom of the Saints*, 149.

When man fails to obtain a hoped-for temporal benefit from God, he falls prey to discouragement and, if left unchecked, he could deem God to be insufficient and, therefore, fall headlong into pursuing worldly aspirations outright.

Shortly after Judas' tragic act of betrayal, the Gospel indicates that "Judas, who betrayed him, seeing that [Jesus] was condemned, repenting himself, brought back the thirty pieces of silver to the chief priest and ancients" (Mt 27:3).

Overwhelmed by guilt, Judas' remorse caused him to repent. Yet, instead of turning to God, he sought forgiveness from the wrong source—the people who cared nothing for him or for Christ.[43] Consequently, Judas, "casting down the pieces of silver in the temple, he departed: and went and hanged himself with an halter" (Mt 27:5).

The halter, a rope harness used to lead a beast of burden such as an ass, symbolizes the Lord's will, that, if a man should accept, he will be led by God and to God. Judas, cast off the halter of God's will, refusing to return to Jesus, and, therefore, this rejection of God's will became the cause of his self-imposed death. The will of God, if accepted, will lead a man to true repentance, to Jesus, while rejecting it leads to guilt and the despair associated with it.

During the Last Supper, after Jesus prophetically foretold, "This very night you will all fall away on account of me" (Mt 26:31, NIV), Peter responded, "Although all shall be scandalized in thee, yet not I. And Jesus saith to him: Amen I say to thee, to day, even in this night, before the cock crow twice, thou shall deny me thrice" (Mk 14:29–30).

43 See *His Tongue Shall Speak Judgment*, Clovis Minor, https://speakjudgment.com/2021/06/04/unmasking-the-man-of-sin.

Later, in the Garden of Gethsemane, as Jesus is being apprehended by the Temple guards, Peter demonstrated his zealous love for Christ and attempted to behead Malchus, the high priest's servant, but, instead, he severed the servant's ear from his head. Peter relentlessly and courageously followed Jesus, even to the high priest's courtyard, in hopes of being close to Jesus during His trial. It was love for Christ that compelled Peter to risk his life in his effort to remain close to Jesus.

However, while warming himself, amidst a charcoal fire, Peter was identified and accused as being one of Jesus' disciples, and, as Christ predicted, Peter renounced his affiliation to Jesus three times. "And Peter going out, wept bitterly" (Lk 22:62).

Peter and Judas both committed grievous sins against our Lord, both repented of their sin, and both fled to isolation, yet Judas placed his hope in men and despaired of God, while Peter clung in faith to Christ and His words: "But I have prayed for thee, that thy faith fail not: and thou, being once converted, confirm thy brethren" (Lk 22:32).

After Christ's Crucifixion, Peter, utterly humiliated, eventually returned to and was received by his brother Apostles. "Things could not have been easy for [Peter]. The story of his denial would soon get about, for people love a malicious tale. It may well be, as legend has it, that people imitated the crow of the cock when he passed. But Peter had the courage and the tenacity of purpose to redeem himself, to start from failure and attain to greatness."[44]

It is important to note that the Gospel of Mark recounts in detail Peter's denial of Christ. Mark was Peter's spiritual son, which

44   William Barclay, *Gospel of John*, 269.

indicates that Peter recounted not only Christ's victories to Mark, but also his own personal failings. It appears that Peter, through Mark, wanted to ensure that the worst of sinners can be transformed by God's mercy into the greatest of saints.

Lord Jesus, burn the image of your holy face into me
that I may become a revelation of your glory,
that I may proclaim as did the holy Apostle:
"It is no longer I who lives but Christ who lives in me." Amen.

Stage 6

Fifth Week of Lent

Testimony and Trials

During this, our second to last stage of our Lenten journey, we return to the foundational themes threaded throughout Jesus' earthly pilgrimage: identity and mission. Indeed, in the face of impending torment, cruel torture, and, ultimately, death on the Cross, Jesus will proclaim His threefold identity as human, divine, and king. It is this fully proclaimed and lived identity that He exchanges for our fallen identity. He bestows upon man His perfect identity, while taking upon Himself the fallen identity of man and the fateful consequences of his rejection of the living God. We continue to accompany Jesus as He embraces our cross, a cross that He claims as His own. By means of increasing charitable contributions, tithing regularly from our gross income, visiting the homebound, infirmed, and lonely, and spending our time to help another with his or her projects, we avail ourselves to God's transformative grace that He may give us His generous heart.

Stage 6 Spiritual Practices
(select two or three)

The purpose of this stage is to develop a generous heart in the image of Jesus' Sacred Heart. Jesus surrendered all that He possessed that we may possess Him and His life. Therefore, we identify ways to be more generous to our neighbors and fellow man, particularly those who have great needs. Truly, the one who gives begins to live.

Make one larger charitable donation to a mission or institution
that works with the less fortunate.

Visit an elderly, sick, or homebound person.

Devote time to assisting someone with a project.

Ensure that you tithe (10%) to your local parish (the tithe should be
based on gross income).

Day 33

(Lent Week 5: Sunday)

INVOCATION: JESUS, THANK YOU FOR MAKING ME WHO I AM.

THE FINAL ASSAULT ON CHRIST'S HUMANITY

Jesus Professes His Human Nature

"Which one of you is Jesus the Nazarene" see John 18:5

R ecall that one's identity leads to his destiny. Man must become who he is truly, who God has created him to be, if he is to attain heaven, the beatific vision.

Saint Thomas Aquinas, in the introduction of his *Summa Theologica*, writes, "Our Lord has taught us that this beatific knowledge has to do with two truths, namely, the divinity of the blessed Trinity and the humanity of Christ. That is why, addressing the Father, He says: 'This is eternal life: that they may know Thee, the only true God, and Jesus Christ, who thou has sent" (Jn 17:3).[45]

Jesus, particularly His human identity and His earthly pilgrimage as the Son of man, is the path we all must endeavor upon to attain

---

45   St. Thomas Aquinas, *Summa Theologica*, Article 2, Book 1.

the beatific vision—the Trinity. To simplify this thought: Jesus is the person and path, particularly His human nature, to our destiny, the Trinity. For this reason, He calls Himself the Way. He, and His life's example, is "the Way" to eternal life in the Most Holy Trinity.

Returning to the theme that began our reflections, Jesus's tenuous battle was to maintain and proclaim His identity in the face of tremendous adversity, overwhelming persecution, and relentlessly hostile intimidation. The salvation of mankind was dependent upon His successful completion of this mission, for Christ, as *the* faithful Son, is *the* representative of the human race, who expresses unfailing trust in His Father. If the Son of God failed to trust and proclaim who He is, none would be capable of becoming sons of God.

The evil one, who began this assault on Jesus' identity during Christ's forty days in the wilderness, circles back, returning to complete his attack on Christ, intending to inflict forceful pressure and suffering upon Him in the hope that Jesus will recoil from His true identity. The evil one's agenda is to ensure that Jesus does not faithfully fulfill His mission of being the Lamb of God, who trusts that His tragic death will be rewarded with victory over the grave.

As mentioned previously, the devil's strategy against Christ was threefold: an attack on Jesus's human identity, Christ's divine identity, and the Lord's kingship. For our purpose, we will concentrate our focus on the evil one's first assault on our Lord's humanity.

As the cohort, led by Judas Iscariot, entered the Garden of Gethsemane, "Jesus therefore, knowing all things that should come upon him, went forth, and said to them: Whom seek ye?' They answered him: Jesus of Nazareth. Jesus saith to them: I am he" (Jn 18:4-5).

In this crucial and pivotal moment, Christ was confronted with the incredible temptation to flee and deny His true identity. Having perfect foreknowledge of all that would befall Him, Jesus comprehended the unspeakable tortures that laid in wait if He chose to confess His human identity—Jesus of Nazareth.

It will be highly beneficial for us to not gloss over this historical moment or proceed too hastily to the following moments of Jesus' Passion, for contained within this event itself are vital lessons that can be applied to every man's life.

Jesus, when prompted to identify Himself—His human nature—refused to flee and resisted the temptation to rely on His supernatural prerogatives and powers to crush His enemy, and instead responded, "I am he." Christ neither succumbed to fear by acting in a pusillanimous manner, nor did He deny His humanity by misusing the power of His divinity.

Overcoming all fear and intimidation, Jesus stepped forward, confessing His human nature, submitting to His Father's Holy Will with perfect resignation, trust, and abandonment.

From the very moment preceding Adam's—our first father's—fall from grace, man has literally attempted to cover his human identity. Man attempts to redeem his "fig leaves," "those garments of misery,"[46] by clothing himself in styles, fashions, brands, and the like. He attempts to convert his sinful shame into his personal glory. Indeed, man has become an expert at covering his humanity with a false artifice of pride.

However, Christ's courageous example summons the Christian man to rise in confidence, embracing, loving, and being thankful for the human nature that he has received from God. In other words, Christ calls us to accept and embrace who we really are, who we have

46   St. Gregory of Nyssa, *https://www.newadvent.org/fathers/2910.htm.*

been created to be, in all humility. St. Teresa of Ávila tells us that *humilitas est Veritas* (humility is truth).[47] When a man is humble, he is truly who he is. By embracing the truth of his humanity, man embraces humility, by embracing humility he embraces truth, and, by embracing the truth of who he is, man becomes who God has called him to be, and, thus, he sets the world ablaze.

The evil one consistently uses people to mock a man's personality, his physical appearance and features, and his emotional disposition for the purpose of having him "cover up" his true self. The evil one knows that if a man masks his true identity, he will never become who God has called and destined him to be, and, therefore, he will become incapable of achieving his destiny of leading others to the beatific vision.

Jesus' admission of His human nature, despite the horrific suffering that would follow, is a testament to the fact that the way to Christian freedom is to embrace the gift of our human nature with great joy and gratitude. It is imperative that a man continually strive to combat all forms of intimidation, shame, and embarrassment launched by the devil upon the gift of his human nature.

If a man embraces his God-given human identity, he will become capable of "going forth" and defending the garden, his domain, woman, and the Church. When a man overcomes the devil's attack on his human nature, he becomes a manifestation and a revelation of the humanity of Christ, who, as the divine bridegroom, loved His bride to the point of laying down His life for her.

My son, only a man, confident that God makes no mistakes, and that his human identity reflects God's image, can glorify God in his

47   St. Thomas Aquinas, Summa Theologica, Book 2, Part 2, Question 161.

body (see 1 Cor 6:20). Therefore, be not ashamed of the man God created you to be. Go forth and glorify God in your body.

Lord Jesus, burn the image of your holy face into me
that I may become a revelation of your glory,
that I may proclaim as did the holy Apostle:
"It is no longer I who live, but Christ who lives in me." Amen.

———

Optional Scripture Readings: John 8:1–12

———

FULFILL YOUR SELECTED SPIRITUAL PRACTICES FROM STAGE 6:
TESTIMONY AND TRIALS.

Day 34

(Lent Week 5: Monday)

INVOCATION: JESUS, THANK YOU FOR YOUR HOLY SPIRIT
DWELLING WITHIN ME.

ASSAULT ON DIVINE IDENTITY

Jesus Professes His Divine Nature

"Art thou then the Son of God?" Luke 22:70

After the Temple guards apprehended Jesus and bound Him, they drug Him from the Garden of Gethsemane and brought Him before the Sanhedrin to be tried.

The Sanhedrin had full legal power over religious matters but did not possess the capacity to inflict the death penalty on anyone. Ultimately, they could only present the criminal and the charges lodged against Him to the ruling Roman government, for the Romans alone had the power to inflict the death penalty.

For a Jewish trial to be valid, a number of prescriptions had to be fulfilled: first, the trial could not occur at night, nor on any feasts; second, the full assembly of all seventy-one members of the Sanhedrin (the ruling class of the Jews comprised of Sadducees, Pharisees, and scribes) must be present; third, witnesses were to be examined individually and privately, and all of the details from their testimony had to agree exactly; fourth, the priest leading the trial could not ask the defendant a leading question because the Law stated that the person on trial could not be forced to incriminate himself; fifth, the Sanhedrin must convene in the Hall of Hewn Stone; and sixth, if the verdict was death, a night must elapse before judgment was carried out for the purpose of allowing mercy to be extended.[48]

Considering this, Jesus was unjustly tried. Those conducting the trial flagrantly rejected all of the legal prescriptions that validated a trial.

Jesus' trial occurred at night; the assembly of the Sanhedrin was only in partial attendance; the witnesses were examined publicly, not individually; none of them could agree on the details of the accusations lodged against Jesus; the trial was held in Caiaphas' courtyard rather than in the Hall of Hewn Stone; and Caiaphas, who had reached a point of frustration as the trial spun out of control, not only asked Jesus a leading question but demanded, "I adjure thee by the living God, that thou tell us if thou be the Christ the Son of God" (Mt 26:63). Caiaphas misused and abused His divine prerogative as high priest to juridically demand a response form Jesus, who humbly obeyed. In other words, Caiaphas demanded that Jesus proclaim His divine identity.

The title "son of God," when used in the Old Testament, referred to Israel being YHWH's adopted son.[49] Yet, when this title was applied to Jesus, the meaning and significance of Son of God changed from an adopted son to the actual only Son of God. The title was used

48   See Barclay, *Gospel of John*, 262.
49   See Dictionary of the Bible, 830; see Ex 4:22; Dt 14:1; 32:19; 43:6; Jer 31:9; Hos 2:1; 11:1.

by demoniacs in reference to Jesus (see Mt 8:29; Mk 3:11; 5:7). The title was also used by the Apostles when Jesus exhibited supernatural power (see Lk 4:41; 8:28); it was pronounced in the most dramatic situations (see Mt 16:16; 14:33); and it was the title most solemnly used by God at Jesus' baptism (see Mt 3:17; Mk 1:11; Lk 3:22) and His Transfiguration (see Mt 17:5; Mk 9:7; Lk 9:35; 2 Pt 1:17).[50]

It is in this sense and meaning—Jesus being the only true, begotten Son of God—that Jesus was accused and tried for blasphemy. The specific accusation waged against Christ by the religious authorities was foreshadowed hundreds of years prior to Jesus' earthly existence in the book of Wisdom:

"He boasteth that he hath the knowledge of God, and calleth himself the son of God. He is become a censurer of our thoughts. He is grievous unto us, even to behold: for his life is not like other men's and his ways are very different. We are esteemed by him as triflers, and he asbstaineth from our ways as from filthiness, and he preferreth the latter end of the just, and glorieth that he hath God for his Father. Let us see then if his words be true, and let us prove what shall happen to him, and we shall know what his end shall be. For if he be the true son of God, he will defend him, and will deliver him from the hand of his enemies. Let us examine him by outrages and tortures, that we may know his meekness, and try his patience. Let us condemn him to a most shameful death: for there shall be respect had unto him by his words. These things they thought, and were deceived: for their own malice blinded them. (Wis 2:13–21)

Indeed, as Jesus triumphantly entered Jerusalem riding on an

50   Ibid.

ass, "the Pharisees therefore said among themselves: Do you see that we prevail nothing? Behold, the whole world is gone after him" (Jn 12:19). "If we let him alone, so all will believe in him; and the Romans will come, and take away our place and nation" (Jn 11:48). To which "Caiaphas, being the high priest that year, said to them: You know nothing. Neither do you consider that it is expedient for you that one man should die for the people and the whole nation perish not" (Jn 11:49–50), and "from that day therefore they desired to put [Jesus] to death" (Jn 11:53).

Jesus, in the face of outrages and tortures, overcame all temptation to deny His divine nature and, instead, confessed that He is the true son of God and that He has God for His Father. Submitting to Caiaphas the high priest's authority, Jesus responded to his question by making the great confession, "I am" (Mk 14:62).

Notice that Jesus, though He is God the Son, submits to the authority of God's anointed, the high priest. Though Christ has ultimate authority as God, He submits to the authority of God vested in one who misuses that power.

Not only does our Lord admit that He is God's only Son, but He also indicated that He is God the Son. The title "I AM WHO I AM" is the ineffable name, the solemn expression of God's identity that He gave to Moses, and "by this name God will be invoked over the centuries."[51] Yet, "it is under this title that the divinity of Jesus will be acclaimed: 'Jesus is LORD'" (CCC 209).

Indeed, Jesus proclaimed His divine identity prior to His trial before the Jews by saying, "Before Abraham was made, I AM. They took up stones therefore to cast at him" (Jn 8:58–59). "The Jews answered him: For a good work we stone thee not, but for blasphemy:

---

51 Navarre Bible Commentary, *Pentateuch* (Princeton, NJ: Scepter Publishing Inc., 257.

and because that thou, being a man, make thyself God" (Jn 10:33).

Because you, my son, are a baptized Christian, you are a temple of God, and the Spirit of God dwelleth in you (see 1 Cor 3:16; CCC 1265), the evil one, as He did with Christ, will afflict you and tempt you to be ashamed of your divine sonship. He will intimidate you in hopes that you will not pray in public, that you will not proclaim your fidelity and belief in Jesus as Lord, and that you will not allow "your light shine before men, that they may see your good works, and glorify your Father who is in heaven" (Mt 5:16).

Therefore, Jesus warns us sternly, "For he that shall be ashamed of me and of my words, of him the Son of man shall be ashamed, when he shall come in his majesty and that of his Father and of the holy angels" (Lk 9:26). Indeed, my son, Christ bore the shame of your sin in His humanity, that you might become a bearer of the light of His divine glory.

Lord Jesus, burn the image of your holy face into me
that I may become a revelation of your glory,
that I may proclaim as did the holy Apostle:
"It is no longer I who live, but Christ who lives in me." Amen.

Optional Scripture Readings: Wisdom 2:13–21; Luke 22:64–71;
Matthew 26: 59–68; John 8:24–39

FULFILL YOUR SELECTED SPIRITUAL PRACTICES FROM STAGE 6:
TESTIMONY AND TRIALS.

Day 35

(Lent Week 5: Tuesday)

INVOCATION: JESUS, NEVER ALLOW ME TO
BETRAY YOU WITH HYPOCRISY.

RELIGIOUS HYPOCRISY

The Jews Take Jesus Before Pilate

———

"They led Jesus from [Caiaphas] to the
governor's hall." John 18:28

"Then they led Jesus from [Caiaphas] to the governor's hall. And it was morning: and [the Pharisees] went not into the hall, that they might not be defiled, but that they might eat the pasch" (Jn 18:28).

As mentioned previously, Caiaphas and the Pharisees transgressed nearly every legal prescription regarding the trial of Jesus. Indeed, the Law stated that, if the accused was found guilty and the verdict was death, at least a full night must elapse before judgment could be carried out for the purpose of affording the Sanhedrin the opportunity to change its verdict and extend mercy to the accused. Even this, the Jewish authorities defied, hastily herding Jesus to

Pilate for the purpose of obtaining a death sentence, while they, in a spirit of religious self-righteousness, partook in the Passover.

John, in his Gospel, highlights that, though the Pharisees flagrantly defied the precepts concerning a proper and just trial, they "went not into [Pilate's] hall, that they might not be defiled, but that they might eat the pasch [the Passover meal] (Jn 18:28).

To eat the Passover, a Jew had to be absolutely ceremonially clean. Now, if they had gone into Pilate's headquarters, they would have incurred uncleanness in a double way. First, the scribal law said, 'The dwelling places of Gentile are unclean; Second, the Passover was the Feast of Unleavened Bread. Part of the preparation for it was a cere-monial search for leaven, and the banishing of every particle of leaven from every house because it was the symbol of evil. To [enter] Pilate's headquarters would have been to [enter] a place where leaven might be found; and to go into such a place when the Passover was being prepared was to render oneself unclean.[52]

Those condemning Christ meticulously observed the ceremo-nial rituals demanded for the Passover for the purpose of main-taining spiritual purity, while the filth of envy, malice, and the murder of Christ occupied their motivations. Indeed, they assem-bled to worship, while neglecting the Spirit of the one Whom they worshipped. The Pharisees followed the letter of the Law, while avoiding the spiritual reasons for the Law. "For the letter killeth: but the spirit quickeneth" (2 Cor 3:6). They rigorously obeyed the disciplines of men, while being intent on crucifying the Son of God.

---

52 Barclay, *Gospel of John*, 274.

As Christ said, "Ye leave the commandment of God, and hold fast the tradition of men" (Mk 7:8, ASV)

This hypocritical dynamic continues even to this day. Many partake in the New Pasch, the Lords' Supper, as a fulfillment of the Church's precept, yet proceed to carry out their own pursuits on the Lord's Day (see Is 58:13). We receive our Lord's Body and Blood, yet with those same tongues we slander and detract our brothers. We ensure that women dress modestly for Mass while their breasts and legs are revealed the rest of the week. We tithe to the Church and yet ignore the homeless and the poor. We recite memorized prayers, while thinking of nearly anything but the God to whom we are addressing. Of these, our Lord speaks harshly, "This people honoureth me with their lips: but their heart is far from me" (Mt 15:8).

We receive the unfathomable mercy in the sacrament of Confession from the God against whom we have sinned and yet condemn those who have sinned against us. We appeal to God for forgiveness, while refusing to forgive. We avoid adultery yet lust in our hearts.

Woe to us, for we "have left the weightier things of the law: judgment and mercy and faith" (Mt 23:23). By doing these things, we become "blind guides, who strain out a gnat and swallow a camel" (Mt 23:24). We become obsessed with trivial matters of disciplines and rubrics without disciplining ourselves. We appear outwardly just, "but inwardly [we] are full of hypocrisy and iniquity (Mt 23:28).

The fact that the Pharisees' hypocrisy is revealed in the context of their observance of the legal prescriptions for the Passover is very important to men of our own age. The Pharisees condemn the one from whom they ought to have sought mercy. A man who receives God's mercy and yet fails to be merciful risks condemnation. A man who uses the law to justify himself is condemned by the law, for no man can fulfill the law perfectly. "For if justice be by the law, then Christ died in vain" (Gal 2:21), for "in the law no man is justified" (Gal 3:11).

The New Passover is the promise of Jesus' mercy extended to us throughout the ages. Therefore, if we receive Christ, we are to be Christ. If we receive His mercy, we ought to extend it to others. As St. Thomas penned, "Faith will tell us Christ is present, even when our senses fail."[53] It is imperative that we recognize the merciful Christ present in the Eucharist and, also, in those we struggle to love. The more that we have faith in the former, the more will we perceive God in the latter.

Lord Jesus, burn the image of your holy face into me
that I may become a revelation of your glory,
that I may proclaim as did the holy Apostle:
"It is no longer I who lives but Christ who lives in me." Amen.

———

Optional Scripture Readings: John 18:12–35; Matthew 23:1–39

———

FULFILL YOUR SELECTED SPIRITUAL PRACTICES FROM STAGE 6:
TESTIMONY AND TRIALS.

---

53   St. Thomas Aquinas, *Pange lingua*: *"Præstet fides suppleméntum sénsuum deféctui."*

+ JMJ +

Day 36

(Lent Week 5: Wednesday)

INVOCATION: JESUS, GIVE ME THE GRACE TO
RECEIVE MY KINGSHIP IN YOU.

KINGLY IDENTITY

Jesus Is Interrogated by Pilate

"Art thou the king of the Jews?" Luke 23:3

Recall that threaded throughout Jesus' Passion narrative is the central theme of His battle to maintain and proclaim His true identity.

The third satanic assault—waged through the medium of the Roman cohort—was precisely upon Jesus' kingship. Pilate, interrogating Jesus asked Him, "Art thou the king of the Jews? (Jn 18:33). "Jesus answered: My kingdom is not of this world. If my kingdom were of this world, my servants would certainly strive that I should not be delivered to the Jews: but now my kingdom is not from hence'" (Jn 18:36). Pilate responded, "You are a king, then!" (Jn 18:37, NIV). "Then therefore Pilate took Jesus and scourged him" (Jn 19:1). "And stripping him, they put a scarlet cloak about him. And platting a crown of thorns, they put it upon his head, and a reed in his right hand. And bowing the knee before him, they mocked him, saying: Hail, King of the Jews. And spitting upon him, they took the reed and struck his head" (Mt 27:28–30).

A torrent of evil had been unleashed upon Jesus for the purpose of dethroning Him from His divine kingship. Yet, "they dug a pit before my face, and they are fallen into it" (Ps 57:6), for, by assaulting Jesus' kingship, the cohort provided Christ the opportunity to express the paradoxical and mysterious nature of His divine headship.

The Roman cohort of soldiers crowned with thorns the Creator Who created man as crown of His creation (see Ps 8). Placing a mock scepter in His right hand, the soldiers defied the One who "shalt rule them with a rod of iron" (Ps 2:9). With ridicule, Pilate's men genuflected before the One at whose name "every knee should bow, of those that are in heaven, on earth, and under the earth" (Phil 2:10). The soldiers smote the Head Who has divine authority over the body of believers (see Eph 5:23). This scornful derision of Christ's kingship allowed Christ the opportunity to display true kingship fully, which is rooted in self-mastery for the sake of self-donation.

The world's version of kingship is characterized by tyranny, domination, display of power, suppression, and oppression, whereas Jesus' kingship is expressed by His elevation of His subjects, a sharing of His divine glory with mortal man.

Rather than dominating another, Christ shares His dominion with the other (see Gen 1:28; Ps 8:7–9). Our Lord demonstrates that a true king who subjects his passions is worthy of his subjects. A king who masters himself is worthy of being recognized as master. A king who rules his power is capable of ruling with power, without his power ruling him.

Jesus teaches us the lesson of true headship: To give power one must possess power, and to possess power one must possess himself, and one can only possess himself by allowing God to possess him and his passions. To rule others, a king must first rule himself. To master his kingdom, a king must be master of himself, for a leader cannot give to his subjects what he does not first possess.

That man is rightly called a king who makes his own body an obedient subject and, by governing himself with suitable rigor, refuses to let his passions breed rebellion in his soul, for he exercises a kind of power over himself. And because he knows how to rule his own person as king, so too does he sit as its judge. He will not let himself be imprisoned by sin or thrown headlong into wickedness."[54] (CCC 908)

See how different God's version of kingship is than the version of kingship that the world proposes. The worldly ruler believes that to rule with passion is to indulge his passions. Though he attempts to control the peoples, he can hardly control himself.

Indeed, the spirit of Christ's kingship is paradoxically displayed and expressed by His ruling of Himself. If you desire to be a leader in the image of Christ, it is necessary that you rule yourself by allowing Christ to reign from within you. It is through Baptism that God the King dwells in us, making us true kings in the King of kings.

We who are baptized in Christ are "heirs indeed of God and joint heirs with Christ" (Rom 8:17) and "are made sharers in . . . the priestly, prophetic, and kingly office of Christ"[55] (CCC 897).

---

54 St. Ambrose, *Psal.* 118:14:30:PL 15:1476.
55 *Lumen Gentium*, 31.

Therefore, "be not conformed to this world: but be reformed in the newness of your mind, that you may prove what is the good and the acceptable and the perfect will of God" (Rom 12:2).

Kingship in Christ demands a renewal of our minds to think with the mind of Christ. The divine king is not satisfied with looking down upon His subjects for the purpose of elevating Himself, but rather He intentionally lowers Himself beneath all, that all, on the day of His Resurrection, may be lifted by Him to His God and Father.

My son, a true leader and king of his family does not look down on his subjects but rather lowers himself in service to them that they may be lifted up to God.

Lord Jesus, burn the image of your holy face into me
that I may become a revelation of your glory,
that I may proclaim as did the holy Apostle:
"It is no longer I who live, but Christ who lives in me." Amen.

Optional Scripture Readings: John 18:33–37;
Luke 23:1–4; Romans 8: 12–18; Psalm 8

FULFILL YOUR SELECTED SPIRITUAL PRACTICES FROM STAGE 6:
TESTIMONY AND TRIALS.

Day 37

(Lent Week 5: Thursday)

INVOCATION: JESUS, THANK YOU FOR
RANSOMING ME FROM MY PERDITION.

THE RANSOM

Jesus Is Judged by Pilate

"Not this man, but Barabbas." John 18:40

"Now upon the solemn day the governor was accustomed to release to the people one prisoner, whom they would. And he had then a notorious prisoner that was called Barabbas. They therefore being gathered together, Pilate said: Whom will you that I release to You: Barabbas, or Jesus that is called Christ?" (Mt 27:15–17)

"But the whole multitude together cried out, saying: Away with this man, and release unto us Barabbas. (Lk 23:18)

Up to this point, Jesus had steadfastly professed His threefold identity: His human nature as Son of man, His divine nature as Son of God, and His kingship as Lord of all. In this pivotal moment, when Pilate "brought Jesus forth and sat down in the judgment seat, in the place that is called Lithostrotos, and in Hebrew Gabbatha" (Jn 19:13), Jesus' identity and mission converge.

Now that He had testified to His identity, Jesus purposefully willed to exchange His identity with a fallen man. Barabbas was a notorious revolutionary, a murderer, whose name literally meant "Son of the Father." Additionally:

> Barabbas was also called Jesus. Some of the very oldest versions of the New Testament, for example the Syriac and Armenian versions call him Jesus Barabbas; and those early interpreters of Scripture, Origen, and Jerome, both knew of that reading and felt it might be correct. It is a curious thing that twice Pilate refers to Jesus who is called the Christ (verse 17 and 22 [of Matthew]) as if to distinguish him from some other Jesus. . . . And the dramatic shout of the crowd most likely was: "Not Jesus Christ, but Jesus Barabbas!"[56]

During this moment, the just judge allowed Himself to be judged unjustly. He who committed no crime exchanged Himself with the criminal. He who came not to condemn (see Jn 3:17) surrendered Himself to be condemned. Jesus took upon Himself the merciless judgment that man deserved that man may begin to believe and trust that God is merciful.

Indeed, Jesus Barabbas, the criminal, the revolutionary, is a rich symbol of fallen mankind— rebellious children who have squandered their identity and inheritance as sons of God the Father. Jesus exchanged His identity as the sinless, faithful Son with the fallen,

---

56 Barclay, *Gospel of Matthew Commentary*, 422.

rebellious, sinful son, to ensure that the slave to sin may be set free by Him who became sin for us, though He had not sinned (see 2 Co 5:21). "Christ also died once for our sins, the just for the unjust: that he might offer us to God" (1 Pt 3:18).

Often, the religious man calculates his offerings that he makes to God. He measures with exactitude his sacrifices. Yet, Christ did not measure or calculate His offering but rather took on the condemnation of Barabbas—a symbol of all fallen sons of the Father who had become criminals in the sight of God.

This raises the question: How could God be just by allowing us, who are justly deserving of condemnation because of our sins, to be delivered from the justice due for our transgressions?

God allowed, in agreement with His Son, the just recompense for our sins to fall upon Jesus. Christ stood in Barabbas' place—and in our place—to demonstrate "his justice in this time: that he himself may be just and the justifier of him who is of faith of Jesus Christ" (Rom 3:26).

In other words, the Son of God received the full measure of the just consequences of the sins of the sons of men, that the sons of men may have faith in the mercy of the Son of God and the Son's Father. Though Jesus Barabbas was released from his death sentence, he must have eventually understood that Jesus, *Bar Abba*, took that death sentence upon Himself. It is for this reason that no human sacrifice can atone for sins or justify man in the sight of God. Only the sacrifice of the Son of God suffices.

Our Lord Jesus lived what He taught and taught what He lived. By exchanging Himself for Barabbas—and for each of us—He embodies His most glorious teaching, "Greater love than this no man hath, that a man lay down his life for his friends" (Jn 15:13).

The true friend has the same will as his companion. Jesus willed that which we desire truly: to be set free from our captivity to sin and its consequences.

Lord Jesus, burn the image of your holy face into me
that I may become a revelation of your glory,
that I may proclaim as did the holy Apostle:
"It is no longer I who live, but Christ who lives in me." Amen.

Optional Scripture Readings: John 18:37–19:15;
Matthew 27:15–17; Luke 23:1–25

FULFILL YOUR SELECTED SPIRITUAL PRACTICES FROM STAGE 6:
TESTIMONY AND TRIALS.

Day 38

(Lent Week 5: Friday)

INVOCATION: JESUS, GIVE ME THE GRACE TO
BE YOUR TRUE FRIEND.

THE CROSS

Jesus Embraces His Cross

———

"And bearing his own cross, he went forth to the
place which is called Calvary." John 19:17

The routine of crucifixion was always the same. When the case had been heard and the criminal condemned, the judge uttered the fateful sentence: "*ibis ad crucem,*" "You will go to the cross . . ." The condemned man was placed in the center of a quaternion, a company of four Roman soldiers. His own cross was placed upon his shoulder. Scourging always preceded crucifixion, and it is to be remembered how terrible scourging was. Often the criminal had to be lashed and goaded along the road, to keep him on his feet, as he staggered to the place of crucifixion. Before him walked an officer with a placard on which was written the crime for which he was to die, and he was led through as many streets as possible on the way to the execution . . . that as many as possible should see and take warning from his fate.[57]

This was Jesus' lot. Yet, God in His divine providence willed that Christ's fate and man's redemption be forever intertwined and associated with the shameful brutality of the Cross. But why?

The cross, the most barbaric and savage form of execution, signifies also a mysteriously profound truth: God, symbolized by the vertical beam—that which descends from and ascends to heaven—encounters mankind, which is signified by the horizontal beam—whose dominion stretches from the east to the west.

The Cross of Jesus Christ communicates the eternal truth that God chooses to encounter man and remains with man, and bears the burdens and consequences of men's sins amidst the most dire and painful circumstances. Ultimately, the Cross symbolizes the friendship between God and man in Jesus Christ.

Recall that friendship, according to St. Thomas Aquinas is *"eandom voluntatem,"* which means "having the same will." Jesus, by carrying the cross of the fallen, guilty Barabbas—the "son of the Father"—and by carrying our cross and making it His own, testifies that He, the true Son of the Father, is man's true friend.

This is highlighted by the fact that John, in his Gospel, says that Jesus went out "bearing *his own* cross." Indeed, Christ claimed our cross, our guilt, and our shame as His own. Jesus took up the burden of the Cross—the physical symbol and the real punishment of our sins—as His own. Indeed, Jesus counted others as better than Himself, bearing their burden as His own (see Phil 2:3–4).

---

57 Barclay, *Gospel of John,* 292.

Friendship, however, if it is to bear the mark of authenticity demands a reciprocal willing of the others' good, a mutual subjection of one another. Jesus, our true friend, bore our burden of sin, that we may learn to bear the burden of other's sins. Christ claims and carries our cross that we may be inspired to claim and carry the Cross of Christ. Jesus by helping us invites us to help Him by helping others.

Not only does Jesus, the true friend, will our good by bearing the burdens of our sins as His own, but also does He summon us to be His true friends by participating in bearing the Cross with Him for the salvation of souls.

While on the bitter road to Calvary, traditionally referred to as "The Way of the Cross," Jesus encountered three examples of true friends who express how we may assist and befriend Christ.

The first friend that Jesus encountered was His Most Holy Mother Mary. According to the venerated "Stations of the Cross," during the fourth station, the faithful commemorate Jesus meeting His most afflicted Mother.

Amidst the chaos, the clamoring crowds, the lashings, and being prodded by the Roman soldiers, Jesus' and His Mother's eyes met. No words between them were spoken. The pangs of her soul pierced the very heart of God. The creature Mary interceded for her Creator; the Mother of God petitioned God the Father to come to the aid of God her Son. The God who assists man was assisted by the prayerful plea of His Holy Mother. Mary is not only known as the Mother of God the Son, the daughter of God the Father, the Bride of the Holy Spirit but, also, the most faithful friend and companion of the Cross-bearer, whose prayers to God were answered.

"And they forced one Simon a Cyrenian, who passed by coming out of the country, the father of Alexander and of Rufus, to take up his cross" (Mk 15:21). This second friend of Jesus, Simon, is the answer to Mary's prayers. Simon, most likely, was coming to Jerusalem to celebrate the Passover but, being caught up in the wild tumult surrounding Jesus, was forced by the Roman soldiers to carry Jesus' Cross. "And as they led him away, they laid hold of one Simon of Cyrene, coming from the country; and they laid the cross on him to carry after Jesus" (Lk 23:26).

Notice that Simon not only takes up Jesus' Cross but follows Jesus while carrying the Cross. The pace is slow, grinding, and grueling, as Jesus repeatedly faltered and fell. As Simon followed the all-but-dead body of Jesus, he becomes knitted to the soul of Christ. It is precisely through the sharing of Jesus' Cross that Simon becomes Jesus' friend. This Simon is given the "talent" that Simon Peter squandered. Simon Peter fled from the Cross of Christ, while Simon of Cyrene carried Christ's Cross.

Simon of Cyrene teaches us that to be a true friend of Jesus is to take up our cross and follow at the pace that Christ's mandates. This pace is willed by God for our patience, perseverance, and ultimate perfection.

Truly, the sincere nature of Simon the Cyrene's friendship with Jesus is verified by the fact that his two sons, Rufus and Alexander, who later become important figures in the early Christian Church (see Rom 16:13). The bearing of Christ's Cross enabled Simon to become a spiritual father who transmitted the salvation Christ won for mankind to his own children.

The third friend of Christ is the "great multitude of people and of women, who bewailed and lamented him" (Lk 23:27). The expression of true sorrow for another's tribulation is a great solace and proof of authentic compassion and friendship. Yet, Christ consoled those who consoled Him: "Weep not over me; but weep for yourselves and for your children" (Lk 23:28). Rather than allowing the women to focus on Himself, Christ redirects them to focus on themselves. Compassion literally means to share suffering. The compassionate one forgets his sufferings by focusing on the sufferings of others.

Indeed, to be a true friend of Jesus is to be like Mary, who aids Jesus and His body of believers by her zealous prayers; to be like Simon, who assists Jesus by physically bearing His burdens, and the burdens of His body of believers; and to be like the consoling women of Jerusalem by expressing heartfelt compassion and companionship to Jesus and His body of believers amidst the most severe trials.

Lord Jesus, burn the image of your holy face into me
that I may become a revelation of your glory,
that I may proclaim as did the holy Apostle:
"It is no longer I who live, but Christ who lives in me." Amen.

Optional Scripture Readings: John 19:16–17;
Luke 23:26–31; Philippians 2:1–8

FULFILL YOUR SELECTED SPIRITUAL PRACTICES FROM STAGE 6:
TESTIMONY AND TRIALS.

Day 39

(Lent Week 5: Saturday)

INVOCATION: JESUS, GIVE ME THE GRACE
TO NEVER BE ASHAMED OF YOU.

THE NEW ADAM

Jesus Is Stripped of His Clothing

———

"They stripped him." Matthew 27:28, NIV

Shame is a phenomenon that every man, regardless of genetic pedigree, sex, age, or social strata experiences. "Shame is so acute as to cause a fundamental disquiet in the whole human existence."[58]

The experience of shame is directly associated with and encountered in the human body—precisely, the naked exposed body. "Man is ashamed of his body because of lust. In fact, he is ashamed not so much of his body as precisely of lust."[59]

While shame may be experienced in the body, it is not experienced in solitude (unless one is doing something shameful); rather,

---

58 *Theology of the Body* (TOB), 17.
59 Ibid., 116.

shame is manifest when a person's body falls under the gaze and scrutiny of another, is analyzed by another, and is perceived as an object to be objectified or ridiculed.

Shame is the consequence of lust, which attempts to divorce love from sacrifice. "Lust passes on the ruins of the matrimonial significance of the body and . . . aims directly . . . to satisfy only the sexual need of the body."[60]

Shame, though experienced as a kind of evil, is the protection of ones' dignity, a self-defense to the threat of being the object of utilitarian lust. Shame also indicates a "certain 'echo' of man's original innocence itself; a 'negative' . . . of the image, whose 'positive' had been precisely original innocence."[61]

The original primordial experience of man was absent of shame: "And they were both naked: to wit, Adam and his wife: and were not ashamed" (Gen 2:25). Original nakedness is key to understanding man and to comprehending God's plan for man and his original experience prior to the Fall. The fact that Adam and Eve felt no shame in the presence of the other's nakedness indicates that they were not bound by lust but free to love the other without being compelled to use or objectify the other.

They "see and know each other, in fact, with all the peace of the interior gaze, which precisely creates the fullness of intimacy of persons."[62] "The fact that they are not ashamed means the woman was not an 'object' of the man, nor he for her."[63] Absence of lust is absence of shame, which affords the presence of peace in the human soul.

60 Ibid., 149.
61 Ibid., 204.
62 Ibid., 57.
63 Ibid., 75.

The body, far from being perceived as an object of lust, in the original experience, was an object of holiness that fulfilled the divine intention of communicating the image of God.

God said, "Let us make man to our image and likeness" (Gen 1:26). The "us" indicates a divine "We," which we have come to understand as the Most Holy Trinity: three divine Persons whose essence is One. The one God is an eternal exchange of love and an intersubjective exchange of divine Persons (see CCC 221), who are literally in and one with the other.

The "attributes" of the Triune Godhead can be identified as distinction, unity, and fruitfulness. The three distinct Persons are essentially One in unity, and the eternal consequence of this unity is life, love, bliss, rapture, and ecstasy.

Revealed in the body of man and woman is the unique distinct persons as male and female and the expressing of their fundamental need to unite with one another, particularly in the one-flesh union and to be fruitful and multiply, and this fruitfulness is a bodily expression of union and joy.

Therefore, God intended from the beginning that His glory—the self-giving love and life of the intersubjective love of the Trinity—be reflected, revealed, and relived in and through the human body and the one-flesh union.

Yet, after partaking of the forbidden fruit, "the eyes of them both were opened: and when they perceived themselves to be naked, they sewed together fig leaves, and made themselves aprons" (Gen 3:7).

When God alerted Adam that He is aware of the original man's fall from grace, Adam responded, "I was afraid, because I was naked, and I hid myself (Gen 3:10). Indeed, the glory of Adam's nakedness had become his shame.

+ JMJ +

Shame enters when man "realized for the first time that his body ceased drawing upon the power of the spirit, which raised him to the level of the image of God."[64]

From this point, Adam, and the son of Adam, cover themselves with fig leaves, "those garments of misery,"[65] as a testimony that they lack the glory of God. Because of this, man is afraid of revealing himself. He hides under the cloak of "fig leaves," which he has made fashionable and prideful.

After ascending Mount Calvary, they stripped Jesus of His clothes. During this moment, Jesus, in his naked body, revealed and reflected simultaneously both the image of man's sin and the image of the perfect unselfish man. While naked, Jesus becomes the symbol of Adam, putting on full display the interior leprosy of sin as manifested in His scourged, marred flesh, while also showing Himself to be the new unashamed, tender, disinterested (unselfish) Adam, who reveals in his naked body the glory and image of God and His love.

Jesus' naked body is the revelation of the divine bridegroom who transmits love to His bride, the Church, without lust, that is, without any selfish ambition. Christ's naked body speaks of the complete gift of self—self-donation—without any appropriation of the other.

"Christ who was stripped naked on the Cross, and by His nakedness put off from Himself the principalities and powers, and openly triumphed over them on a tree."[66]

From the height of Mount Calvary, Jesus shows Himself to be

64 Ibid., 115.
65 St. Gregory of Nyssa.
66 Cyril of Jerusalem, *Mystagogical, Catechesis*, Lecture 20, 2.

both the fulfillment of Barabbas who has taken upon Himself the death sentence owed to mankind; and the fulfillment of Adam who bears the wounds of sin in His naked flesh, while also being the divine Bridegroom, who tenderly summons His bride, the Church, to union with Him.

My son, the true man crucifies his lusts to the Cross of Christ, and, by means of his genuine "gift of self, "this is my body given for you," he, like Christ, expels demons, conquers hell's dominion, and reigns with Christ. Shame has no power over him, for God's sacrificial love is revealed in and through his body.

Lord Jesus, burn the image of your holy face into me
that I may become a revelation of your glory,
that I may proclaim as did the holy Apostle:
"It is no longer I who lives but Christ who lives in me." Amen.

Optional Scripture Readings: Genesis 3:5–12; Matthew 27:24–30

FULFILL YOUR SELECTED SPIRITUAL PRACTICES FROM STAGE 6: *TESTIMONY AND TRIALS.*

+ JMJ +

Stage 7

Holy Week

LOVE AND LEGACY

During this seventh and final stage of our Lenten journey, Jesus invites us to remain with Him at the foot of the Cross. Suspended between heaven and earth, Jesus transforms His execution into a profound moment of teaching—of mercy. From this pulpit, He associates Himself with the criminal, the rebel; He bestows to man His Holy Mother; He proclaims His triumph over evil; He summons us to quench the thirsty heart of the One who is Living Water; and He imparts to us the promise of paradise and finalizes His mission by entrusting His spirit to His loving Father. By means of intentionally forgiving those and blessing those daily who have offended, betrayed, wounded, or injured us; by asking forgiveness from those whom we have injured; by praising God for the talents and gifts in others that we are jealous or envious of; and by praying for our enemies, we invite Christ's radical merciful forgiving love to enter us that we may enter eternal life.

STAGE 7 SPIRITUAL PRACTICES
(SELECT TWO OR THREE)

By overcoming all bitterness, resentment, and lack of forgiveness lodged secretly deep in our hearts, this stage affords us the opportunity to imitate Christ who said from the Cross, "Father, forgive them, for they know not what they do" (Lk 23:34). By forgiving as Christ forgives, we will find our freedom in Him.

—————

Forgive someone who has betrayed, offended,
or wounded you by asking God to bless them daily.

—————

Ask forgiveness, in person, by phone, or by letter from someone
whom you have injured, offended, wounded, or betrayed.

—————

Praise and thank God specifically for the talents and gifts
that you are jealous or envious of in a certain individual.

—————

Intentionally pray for God's blessing and salvation for an enemy,
or someone your dislike or find disagreeable.

—————

Forgive yourself, believing that God has forgiven you
(for you are to love your neighbor as yourself).

Day 40

(Lent Week 6: Palm Sunday)

<small>INVOCATION: JESUS, THANK YOU FOR BECOMING SIN,
THAT I MAY BECOME ONE WITH YOU.</small>

THE CRIMINAL

Jesus Is Crucified Among Two Thieves

―――――

"And with the wicked he was reputed." Mark 15:28

"And when they were come to the place which is called Calvary, they crucified him there: and the robbers, one on the right hand, and the other on the left" (Lk 23:33). "And the scripture was fulfilled, which saith: And with the wicked he was reputed" (Mk 15:28; see Is 53:12).

Crucifixion was a most cruel and torturous from of execution, "which was not inflicted on Roman citizens; it was reserved for slaves or for non-Romans who had committed heinous crimes such as murder, robbery, and piracy, treason, and rebellion."[67]

―――――

67   *Dictionary of the Bible*, 161.

The cross carried by Jesus to the place of execution, according to customary procedure, was not the entire cross, but only the cross beam. As a rule, the upright beam was left permanently at the place of execution. The arms of the criminal were first attached to the crossbeam, while he was stretched flat on the ground; he was then elevated together with the crossbeam to the upright beam, and his feet were fastened to the upright beam. The fastening was done with by ropes or by nails; if nails were used, four were employed.... Most of the weight of the body was supported by a peg (Latin *sedile*, "Seat") projecting from the upright beam on which the victim sat astride."[68]

During Jesus' lifetime, it was customary, when a ruler or king spoke with authority, he did so while sitting on a throne or chair, as when Pilate sentenced Jesus, or as when Christ delivered His Sermon on the Mount: "When [Jesus] was set down, his disciples came unto him" (Mt 5:1). Jesus used the *sedile* of the Cross as His seat of authority from which He proclaimed His final and most compelling proclamation of His Gospel.

Men intuitively respect those who sacrifice themselves for the sake of others and are inspired by their example to sacrifice themselves for those whom they respect. Indeed, the only trustworthy preacher is the one who teaches from the "seat of sacrifice."

As Jesus' hands and feet were fastened by nails to the wood of the Cross, the helpless victim became the Helper most powerful. Though His physical freedom was fixed to the beams of the Cross, it is, nevertheless, from this Cross that Jesus freely preached the words that will liberate men of every age from the domination of sin.

68   Ibid., 162.

Christ's Gospel, as proclaimed from the pulpit of the Cross, is most believable, for He cannot be perceived as having anything to gain. His only motivation is to procure man's salvation.

Yet, there is another reason for us to believe Jesus' final Gospel proclamation: He does not preach "down" to man, as if He is above man. Jesus chose to be crucified between two sinful criminals, and it is from this seat among sinners that Jesus interceded for them, pleading, "Father, forgive them, for they know not what they do" (Lk 23:34). Situated among sinners, Jesus is able to beg on behalf of corrupt man for his forgiveness, and God cannot refuse His Son's most humble request. Jesus lived what He preached and preached what He lived: "Love your enemies: do good to them that hate you: and pray for them that persecute and calumniate you" (Mt 5:44). It is at this moment that His words are fulfilled: "Unless the grain of wheat falling into the ground die, Itself remaineth alone. But if it die it bringeth forth much fruit" (Jn 12:24–25).

Christ crucified at the center of two criminals hearkens back to a clarifying moment in Jesus' public ministry when our Lord called Levi to abandon his post as a publican and follow Him. Levi (Matthew), after receiving the summons to follow Christ, hosted a celebration at his home, where Jesus and His Apostles gathered with those identified by the Jewish leaders as sinners. Indeed, they asked, "Why doth your master eat with publicans and sinners?" (Mt 9:11).

To which Jesus responded, "Go then and learn what this meaneth, I will have mercy and not sacrifice. For I am not come to call the just, but sinners" (Mt 9:13).

The scribes and Pharisees interpreted righteousness with God to be obtained by separating oneself from the wicked (see Ps 26:4; Prv

4:14), a strict adherence to the legal prescriptions that upheld the Law, and repeated sacrificial offerings.

Eventually, the psychology of right relationship with YHWH was perverted by spiritual self-reliance, the idea that man could actually procure approval and atonement from God by means of his own merits. This, of course, is pride. "For if justice be by the law, then Christ died in vain (Gal 2:21).

"The Lawgiver was not unaware that the burden of the Law exceeded the powers of men. But he judged this useful so men might become aware of their own insufficiency. Therefore, in commanding impossible things, God made men humble. Because, truly, none of us will ever be justified in God's sight by works of the law."[69]

Jesus' first proclamation from the pulpit of the Cross, "Father, forgive them, for they know not what they do" (Lk 23:34) is the expressed depth of God's unfathomable mercy: He forgives those who were the cause of His execution—which is all of us.

In the end, there exist two types of persons: those who live by mercy, and those who live by self-reliance. Only the one who is merciful can communicate with the mercy of Christ, for mercy is His language. If a man attempts to speak with God, using any other language than divine mercy, his prayers and sacrifices are empty, void of God's spirit, and, most certainly, will be rejected.

To be holy is not to be separated from or above sinners but rather to recognize that if Christ associated Himself with and interceded for the sinners who caused His death, we also ought to be with Christ and sinners, for we have caused His death. Indeed, we are

---

69   St. Bernard of Clairvaux, *Ralph Martin, The Fulfillment of All Desire*, Steubenville, Ohio, Emmaus Road Publishing.

sinners who depend on God's mercy and, therefore, are obligated to extend the mercy we have received from God to fellow sinners (see Eph 4:29–32).

My son, remember the dust from which you came. If Christ, who is infinitely greater than you, associates and communes with you a sinner, how can you, a sinner, believe yourself to be so great as to not associate with and forgive sinners?

Lord Jesus, burn the image of your holy face into me
that I may become a revelation of your glory,
that I may proclaim as did the holy Apostle:
"It is no longer I who lives but Christ who lives in me." Amen.

———————

Optional Scripture Readings: Luke 23:32–43; John 12:23–32;
Matthew 9:9–13; Ephesians 4:29–32

———————

FULFILL YOUR SELECTED SPIRITUAL PRACTICES FROM STAGE 7:
LOVE AND LEGACY.

Day 41

(Lent Week 6: Monday)

<small>INVOCATION: JESUS, THANK YOU FOR GIVING ME
YOUR MOST HOLY MOTHER.</small>

BEHOLD YOUR MOTHER

Jesus Gives Mankind His Mother

———

"Behold thy mother." John 19:27

"When Jesus therefore had seen his mother and the disciple standing whom he loved, he saith to his Mother: Woman, behold thy son. After that, he saith to the disciple: Behold thy mother. And from that hour, the disciple took her to his own" (Jn 19:26–27).

The public ministry of Christ that began with His miraculous transformation of water into wine at Cana of Galilee prompted by His Mother's command to the servants, "Do whatever he tells you" (Jn 2:5, NIV), now concludes with her Son's command to His servant John, "Behold thy mother."

To do what Mary commands is to obey her Son's commands, one of which He proclaimed from the pulpit of the Cross, "Behold your mother," which means to "receive her as your own."

John, the beloved disciple, one of Jesus' chosen twelve, was the sole Apostle who, by overcoming the fear of persecution and the possibility of death, courageously ascended Golgotha for the purpose of accompanying his Savior during His last agonizing hours.

John remained close to Mary, who would not suffer to be separated from her Son. Indeed, those like the beloved disciple, who remain close to Mary, cannot and will not be separated from Jesus, for Mary and Jesus are inseparable, as the Scripture says, "The Lord is with [her]" (Lk 1:28).

Remaining by her side, John was the only Apostle to witness the paradoxical apex of Christ's ministry, when the Son of man shall be lifted up in shame, He shall draw all men to Himself in His glory (see Jn 12:32).

John alone witnessed the mystical marriage of the New Adam, Jesus Christ, and the New Eve, Mary. He was a first-hand witness that, through their unique union of wills and mutual consent to suffer for the salvation of sinners, the two gave birth to sons of God, as signified by Christ's command to His Mother, "Behold, your son," that is, another son of God, an *alter Christus*, born from the sacrificial union of Jesus and Mary.

It was through her union of suffering with Christ that God gave Mary new sons in Christ, but we sons also were given a Mother in Mary. John's reward for steadfastly accompanying the Most Holy Virgin during her Son's final moments was the Mother of God herself. At the feet of the agonizing Savior, John took her into his own.

But why should Jesus, during His final moments, command that John and, therefore, all beloved disciples of Christ receive Mary into their own hearts?

Jesus knows that men are either fainthearted or fool hearted, pusillanimous or presumptuous, intimidated by fear of suffering for the Faith, or presume pridefully that they, of their own accord, can procure their own victory. In all cases, the plague of pride metastasizes in the soul of man, preventing him, on one hand, from potential failure, or compelling him toward a victory that God has not yet awarded.

Humility, the lived understanding that apart from God we can accomplish nothing, conditions the soul to depend on God for everything. As the psalmist rejoices, "The Lord is the keeper of little ones: I was humbled [helpless], and he delivered me" (Ps 116:6). This is the proclamation of the humble man. Humility leads to magnanimity—large-heartedness—which is a willingness to generously surrender and give all to God, submitting oneself in full service to Him and His cause.

Humilitas est Veritas (humility is truth), and, in truth, the Blessed Virgin proclaims that she is both the "handmaid of the Lord" (Lk 1:38) and that her "soul doth magnify the Lord" (Lk 1:46). Her humility and lowliness before God enabled her to exude perfect magnanimity, for she is dependent on God to accomplish all that is holy through her.

God cannot help but to glorify the Virgin, whose only goal is to glorify God. She does not presume upon her own glory, but, in her lowliness, she receives it and reveals it. To aid man in successfully and consistently overcoming the sin of pride, Jesus gave him His Mother, for she is the means to conquer pride in all forms.

Foretold at the beginning of salvation history, after Adam and Eve had fallen from grace, having grasped presumptuously for the glory of God, God promised that the Woman and her seed would crush the head of the serpent (see Gen 3:15). This cannot be Eve, for she was tainted by sin. This prophecy can only refer to Mary, the sinless one, the one who Satan cannot conquer, and her seed, her offspring, Jesus.

"The Immaculate alone has from God the victory over Satan. She seeks souls that will consecrate themselves entirely to her, that will become in her hands, forceful instruments for the defeat of Satan and the spread of God's kingdom."[70]

My son, only the humble soul will God exalt, and only the humble will He supply the grace to conquer pride. If you desire to be exalted by God, humble yourself before the Mother of God. If you desire to be a true Christian man, entrust yourself to *the Woman* who crushes the serpent of pride. For if you are to become an effective spiritual father, it is imperative that you receive Mary as your spiritual Mother.

The God who chose not to be created as man without her deemed it necessary to redeem man with her. God, who appointed her to give birth to His Son, has providentially ordained that she, in union with the sacrifice of her Son, give birth to many christs by the gift and power of the Holy Spirit.

Therefore, my son, behold your Mother. Remain, as John did, with Mary, and you will remain with Christ, for the Lord is with her (see Lk 1:28).

---

70 St. Maximilian Kolbe, *https://traditionalcatholicprayers.com/2019/10/06/prayers-of-consecration-to-the-immaculate-heart-of-mary.*

Lord Jesus, burn the image of your holy face into me
that I may become a revelation of your glory,
that I may proclaim as did the holy Apostle:
"It is no longer I who live, but Christ who lives in me." Amen.

———————

Optional Scripture Readings: Genesis 3:15; John 2:1–11;
John 19:25–27; Revelation 12:1–17

———————

FULFILL YOUR SELECTED SPIRITUAL PRACTICES FROM STAGE 7:
LOVE AND LEGACY.

Day 42

(Lent Week 6: Tuesday)

INVOCATION: JESUS, GIVE ME THE GRACE TO BELIEVE
THAT YOUR CROSS IS TRUE TRIUMPH OVER EVIL.

THE FORSAKEN

Christdt Cries Out to His Father

———————

"My God, my God, why hast thou
forsaken me." Matthew 27:46

A s the Savior's human life bled out, the relentless lion, the devil,
sniffing for bodily weakness, pounced upon Jesus with his
re-occurring three-fold attack—a last assault—on Jesus' true identity.

The passersby blasphemed, "Vah, thou that destroyest the temple
of God and in three days dost rebuild it: save thy own self" (Mt
27:40). By saying "save thy own self" and referring to the Temple,
which is Christ's human body, Satan through the bystanders laid
siege against Jesus' human nature.

Again, their words, "if thou be the Son of God, come down from
the cross" (Mt 27:40), was also an attack on Christ's divine nature.
And, "in like manner also the chief priests, with the scribes and

ancients, mocking said . . . if he be the king of Israel, let him now come down from the cross: and we will believe him" (Mt 27:41–42), which was an attack on Jesus' divine kingship. Truly, while on the Cross, Christ's threefold identity comes under fire.

Jesus, to be a perfect sacrificial offering to God, was intent on identifying Himself as sin, though He had sinned not, with the experience of the sinner and with the totality of the experience of abandonment that the sinner experiences when separated from God. Indeed, Jesus deemed it necessary to endure the abandonment caused by sin for the purpose of fully redeeming all sinners.

As Jesus pressed on with the intention to complete His perfect sacrifice and human oblation, the evil one launched his final attack against Jesus' identity, taunting the Savior, tempting Him to prove Himself by delivering Himself from the Cross.

Essentially, the temptation consisted of attempting to convince Jesus that if He did not use His supernatural powers to deliver Himself from His execution, His ministry would end in utter failure, none would continue to believe in Him, and all would be lost.

Yet, Christ, rather than using supernatural prerogatives, responds to the tempters' attack in a manner that has echoed throughout the ages, proving to those present at the Crucifixion and to those who commemorate it, that Jesus is the *human incarnation* of God, that *He is divine*, and that *He is the king* who is sovereign over all creation.

From His seat of authority, Christ cried out, "O God my God . . . why hast thou forsaken me" (Ps 22:1). To the modern ear, this is the expression of absolute defeat. In Jesus' day, however, the utterance of the first sentence of a psalm summons those praying to remember and recite the psalm in its entirety. The first line is like a gunshot that begins the race of recalling the psalm.

Far from a cry of defeat, the words, "O God my God . . . why hast thou forsaken me" was Jesus' recitation of the first line of the prophetic Messianic Psalm 22. By saying the first line of Psalm 22, Jesus was stating that the prophecy contained in the psalm is now fulfilled in Him. Far from being a cry of death, at that very moment, from the Cross, in the face of His nemesis, Christ proclaimed His definitive victory over evil.

The psalms states, "I am a worm, and no man" (Ps 22:6). Christ connects Himself with the figure of the worm, particularly the worm or serpent that Moses fashioned from bronze and fastened to the staff that all who looked upon would be healed. Indeed, all who look upon the Son of Man will be saved (see Jn 6:40).

The psalm continues: "All they that saw me have laughed me to scorn: they have spoken with the lips, and *wagged the head* (Ps 22:7, emphasis added). This is fulfilled in Christ, when "they that passed by blasphemed him, *wagging their heads* (Mt 27:39, emphasis added).

Again, "He hoped in the Lord, *let him deliver him*: let him save him, seeing he delighteth in him' (Ps 22:8, emphasis added) was fulfilled in Christ, "He trusted in God: let him now *deliver him* if he will have him; for he said: I am the Son of God" (Mt 27:43, emphasis added).

Again, "My strength is dried up like a potsherd, and my tongue hath cleaved to my jaws" (Ps 22:15) was fulfilled in Christ when He says from the Cross, "I thirst" (Jn 19:28).

Again, "I am poured out like water; and all of my bones are scattered" (Ps 22:14) was fulfilled in Christ, when "one of the soldiers with a spear opened his side: and immediately there came out blood and water" (Jn 19:34).

"They have dug my hands and feet. They have numbered all my bones" (Ps 22:16–17) was fulfilled by Christ: "For these things were done that the scripture might be fulfilled: You shall not break a bone of him" (Jn 19:36). And again, another scripture says: "They shall look on him whom they pierced" (Jn 19:37).

Again, "They parted my garments amongst them; and upon my vesture they cast lots" (Ps 22:18) was fulfilled in Christ, when, "after they had crucified him, they divided his garments, casting lots; that it might be fulfilled which was spoken by the prophet, saying: They divided my garments among them; and upon my vesture they cast lots" (Mt 27:35).

Again, "And they have looked and stared upon me" (Ps 22:17) was fulfilled in Christ, when "they sat and watched him" (Mt 27:36).

Again, "Deliver, O God, my soul from the sword: my only one from the hand of the dog" (Ps 22:20) was fulfilled in Christ, when "one of the soldiers with a spear opened his side" (Jn 19:34), for the Romans were referred to by the Jews as dogs.

Again, "My heart is become like wax melting" (Ps 22:14) was fulfilled in Christ, when "immediately there came out blood and water" (Jn 19:34).

The Jewish bystanders, especially the scribes and Pharisees, who had memorized the Scriptures, certainly connected the visual reality that was occurring before their eyes with Psalm 22.

Not only does this prophetic psalm foretell the Messiah's trial, but also prophetically declares the glorious triumph of the one who has been pierced. "I will declare thy name to my brethren: in the midst of the church I will praise thee" (Ps 22:22). Christ resurrected lives in the midst of His brethren, where two or three are gathered in His name (see Mt 18:20). Christ in His faithful praises God.

"I will pay my vows in the sight of them that fear him" (Ps 22:25). The Latin word for vow or oath is *sacramentum*. Indeed, the resurrected Christ fulfilled His vow to man, assuring him of His divine grace and salvation, particularly through the sacraments, for "the poor shall eat and shall be filled: and they shall praise the Lord that seek him: their hearts shall live for ever and ever" (Ps 22:26). This promise is the same that Christ gave to His disciples, "I am the living bread which came down from heaven. If any man eat of this bread, he shall live forever" (Jn 6:51) Therefore, "Take ye, and eat. This is my body (Mt 26:26). Do this for a commemoration of me" (Lk 22:19).

Indeed, "all the kindreds of the Gentiles shall adore in his sight (Ps 22:27), and "all they that go down to the earth shall fall before him" (Ps 22:29), for the nations who eat His flesh and drink His blood, He shall "raise [on] the last day" (Jn 6:40).

Christ's cry, "O God my God . . . why has thou forsaken me?" (Ps 22:1) is His definitive proclamation of His true identity and His ultimate victory over the calves that have surrounded him and the fat bulls that have besieged him (see Ps 22:12).

Once again God's logic supersedes man's limited understanding. My son, though the Cross appears to be a tremendous tragedy to the world, if you, like Christ, embrace it, it will be the means of your triumph over the world and its evils.

Lord Jesus, burn the image of your holy face into me
that I may become a revelation of your glory,
that I may proclaim as did the holy Apostle:
"It is no longer I who live, but Christ who lives in me." Amen.

———————

Optional Scripture Readings: Psalm 22; John 19:23–37; Matthew 27:34–50

———————

FULFILL YOUR SELECTED SPIRITUAL PRACTICES FROM STAGE 7:
LOVE AND LEGACY.

Day 43

(Lent Week 6: Wednesday)

INVOCATION: JESUS, GIVE ME THE GRACE TO
BE QUENCH YOUR THIRST FOR SOULS.

THE THIRSTY ONE

Jesus Asks for His Thirst to Be Quenched

"I thirst." John 19:28

Nearing the completion of His human oblation, Jesus raised His all-but-dead body, to allow enough air to enter his lungs and voiced the enigmatic phrase, "I thirst."

On one hand, to any of the bystanders, it was very obvious that he whose "tongue hath cleaved to [his] jaw" (Ps 22:15) was literally dying of thirst. While the simplicity of these words can be taken at face value if we peer beyond the surface of their meaning, we may discover the profound significance of Jesus's divine request.

During the festival of the Tabernacles, or Booths, the priest "took a golden pitcher which held three logs—that is, about two pints—and went down to the Pool of Siloam and filled it with water.

It was carried back through the Water Gate while the people recited Isaiah 12:3, 'With joy you will draw water from the wells of salvation.' The water was carried up to the Temple altar and poured out as an offering to God."[71]

It was on this occasion that Jesus stood in the Temple area and cried aloud, saying, "If any man thirst, let him come to me, and drink. He that believeth in me, as the scripture saith, Out of his belly shall flow rivers of living water. Now this he said of the Spirit which they should receive, who believed in him: for as of yet the Spirit was not given, because Jesus was not yet glorified" (Jn 7:37–39). By making this proclamation during the feast, at this precise liturgical moment, Jesus was signaling to the Jews that if they drink from Him, they will have eternal life.

From the Cross, Jesus, who invites all men to drink from Him—the living water—expressed His thirst. How can He, the living water, who has the ability to quench man's thirst, say that He thirsts? Cannot the one who is living water satisfy his own thirst?

We discover the deeper significance of Christ's plea, "I thirst," when we discover that on another occasion, previously in Jesus' ministry, He expressed this same longing, "I thirst," to the Samaritan woman, during His respite at Jacob's well. It was on this occasion that Jesus asked the Samaritan woman for water, yet she did not supply Him with temporal water. What was it that Jesus was actually thirsting for?

Peering more deeply into the text, we discover that Jesus thirsted for the woman herself, for her response to His summons to faith—

71 Barclay, *Gospel of John Commentary*, 290.

to believe in Him. Jesus longed for the Samaritan woman to drink from Him and to have her thirst for real divine love quenched.

Yet, to awaken the Samaritan woman to her deeper desire for divine love, He exposed her failed attempts to find the love for which she thirsted in men: "For thou hast had five husbands: and he whom thou now hast, is not thy husband" (Jn 4:18). Indeed, she had been with six men, six being a symbol of man being created on the sixth day with the beasts. Jesus, the seventh man—a symbol of the seventh day on which God made a covenant with man—awakened within her a desire and hope that divine love can be attained.

Indeed, her thirst for divine love was quenched by Jesus, for "the woman therefore left her water pot, and went her way into the city, and saith to the men there: Come, see a man who has told me all things whatsoever I have done. Is he not the Christ?" (Jn 4:28–29).

Jesus's plea from the Cross, "I thirst," is His expressed longing that mankind—as with the Samaritan woman—drink from Him, and, by drinking from Him, they might have fountains of living waters welling up within them, waters that will flow to the world around them.

It is interesting to note that, during the festival of Booths, the priest went down to the pool of Siloam to retrieve water to be poured upon the altar of sacrifice. The meaning of the word Siloam means "sent" (see Jn 9:7), which signified that one who will drink from the waters of Christ are commissioned, "sent" to help quench other's thirst for divine love.

But, at the moment of Jesus' encounter with the Samaritan woman, and during His Crucifixion, the Spirit had not yet been given. It seems that for Christ to give man His living water something yet needed to occur. We discover a hint in the prophetic vision of Ezekiel, who was brought by an angel "to the gate of the house [Temple], and behold waters issued out from under the threshold of the house [Temple] toward the east" (Ez 47:1). And the angel said to Ezekiel, "These waters that issue forth toward the hillocks of sand to the east, and go down to the plains of the desert, shall go into the sea, and shall go out, and the waters shall be healed. And every living creature that creepeth whithersoever the torrent shall come, shall live . . . and they shall be healed (Ez 47:8–9).

Ezekiel's prophetic vision is a figure and symbol of the Temple of Christ, the true Water Gate, from whom with joy you will draw water from the wells of salvation. In Ezekiel's vision, water flowed from the side of the Temple, and the living water also flowed from the side of Christ after He was pierced by the Roman soldier's lance.

Additionally, as God brought forth Eve from Adam's side while the first man slept, so also water—the symbol of Baptism—and blood—the symbol of the life of the sacraments—flowed from the Temple of Jesus, giving birth to His bride the Church, as He underwent the sleep of death and His side was opened by a spear. And men, throughout the ages, have been healed by this divine spring.

"I thirst" is the divine plea that all drink from the Temple of Christ be healed and, thus, become a reservoir of grace, so that, being sent (Siloam) to others, they may draw others to the Temple of Christ to be quenched and healed by His life-giving waters.

+ JMJ +

Lord Jesus, burn the image of your holy face into me
that I may become a revelation of your glory,
that I may proclaim as did the holy Apostle:
"It is no longer I who live, but Christ who lives in me." Amen.

Optional Scripture Readings: Psalms 22; John 7:37–39; John 19:23–37

FULFILL YOUR SELECTED SPIRITUAL PRACTICES FROM STAGE 7:
LOVE AND LEGACY.

Day 44

(Lent Week 6: Holy Thursday)

INVOCATION: JESUS, GIVE ME THE GRACE TO LOVE
YOUR MOST HOLY BODY AND BLOOD.

IT IS FINISHED

Jesus Completes His Sacrificial Oblation

———————

"It is Consummated." John 19:30

Man is a being comprised of both spirit and body, and he will be resurrected by God as an integrated whole. Too often, due to a religious scrupulosity and disdain for created matter, man identifies the human body as an evil and misunderstands himself as simply a spiritual—not a corporeal—being. Influenced by Platonic philosophy, many a religious man believes that upon death his spirit will be liberated from the prison of his body and he will spend eternity as a spirit without a body. This notion, however, is contrary to the Gospel.

The Word, though Spirit, became flesh, and, in this flesh, Jesus procured man's salvation by offering His body as a holy and living sacrifice unto God. Therefore, "you are bought with a great price.

Glorify and bear God in your body" (1 Cor 6:20). Every Christian man is obligated to use his body in a manner that glorifies the holy and living God. To glorify God in the body demands that the body be empowered and fed by a glorified body.

Indeed, Christ said, "He that eateth my flesh, and drinketh my blood, hath everlasting life: and I will raise him up on the last day" (Jn 6:54). Jesus connects the reality of the bodily resurrection with the eating of His flesh, His body. Christ identifies Himself as the Bread of Life, living food that purposes to fortify man's body, to ensure that a man be faithful to his mission by offering His body as a holy and living sacrifice unto the Lord (see Rom 12:1).

In other words, if a man is to live a life of sacrifice, he must partake in Christ's living sacrifice, and, if a man's body is to be holy, he must eat the holy Body of the Lord Jesus, for the same body that defeated death and rose from the grave—if a man receives—empowers him to overcome death and experience the bodily resurrection.

From the Cross, as Jesus' prolonged sacrifice drew towards it culminating close, after saying, "I thirst," "they, putting a sponge full of [wine] about hyssop, put it to his mouth. Jesus therefore, when he had taken the [wine], said: It is consummated" (Jn 19:29–30).

As scholars demonstrate, Christ could not be referring to mankind's redemption now being complete, for the Holy Spirit, who makes men sons of God, had not yet been given.[72] In other words, mankind's redemption was not "finished," but rather the sacrifice that began in the Upper Room, at the Pasch, where Christ gave His disciples His Body and Blood to eat, was now completed on Mount Calvary.

---

72 See, for example, Scott Hahn, *The Fourth Cup* (San Diego: Catholic Answers, https://www.catholic.com/magazine/print-edition/hunt-for-the-fourth-cup.

The Passover meal, the Haggadah:

Was divided into four parts, comprised of four cups. First the prelim-
inary course consisted of a festival blessing (kiddush) spoke over the
first cup of wine, followed by the serving of herbs. The second course
included a recital of the Passover narrative and the "Little Hallel"
(Psalm 113), followed by the drinking of the second cup of wine. The
third course was the main meal, consisting of lamb and unleavened
bread, after which was drunk the third cup of wine, known as the "cup
of blessing." The Passover climaxed with the singing of the "Great
Hallel" (Psalms 114–118) and the drinking of the fourth cup of wine. .
. . In particular, the cup blessed and distributed by Jesus is identified as
the third cup in the Passover Haggadah.[73]

Rather than proceeding to the fourth and final cup, Jesus
abruptly abandoned the Passover meal: "And when they had sung
an hymn, they went forth to the mount of Olives" (Mk 14:26).

It was in the garden that Jesus prayed to His Father on three
occasions, "My Father, if it be possible, let this [*cup*] pass from
me. Nevertheless, not as I will but thou wilt" (Mt 26:39, emphasis
added).

Prior to Jesus' Crucifixion, He was offered, "wine mingled with
myrrh" as an opiate to lessen the severity of His excruciating pain,
"but he took it not" (Mk 15:23). But, finally, after realizing that all
was accomplished, He cried out, "I thirst. Now there was a vessel
set there, full of vinegar. And they, putting a sponge full of vinegar
about hyssop, put it to his mouth. Jesus therefore, when he had

73 Ibid.

taken the vinegar, said: It is consummated. And bowing his head, he gave up the ghost" (Jn 19:28-30).

"It was the Passover that was now precisely finished. More precisely, it was Jesus' transformation of the Passover sacrifice of the Old Covenant into the Eucharistic sacrifice of the New Covenant."[74]

What began in the Upper Room, that is, Jesus' Eucharistic sacrifice, was completed on Calvary. By connecting the Last Supper with His sacrifice on Calvary, Christ is communicating that—as John pointed out at the beginning of Jesus' public ministry—He is the Lamb of God (see Jn 1:29), the Passover Lamb (see Ex 12) that takes away the sins of the world (see Jn 1:29), which must be eaten (see Ex 12:4) that the angel of death will pass-over (see Ex 12:13). This is Jesus' identity: the Lamb who was slain yet lives forever (see Rev 5:12).

Jesus' triumphant declaration, "It is finished," is ironically His proclamation that "it has commenced." That which Jesus completed, the sacrifice of God's Lamb, from the Last Supper to this very day is commemorated by Catholics at every Holy Sacrifice of the Mass by eating the Lamb of God. Man eats of the Lamb that he may fulfill his mission to become another lamb who follows the True Shepherd to his final end.

Indeed, the Lamb's flesh and blood become "food for the journey" that enables us to fulfill our mission and experience the bodily resurrection. My son, by means of the Eucharist, Christ's sacrificial death lives in you, that you may live in God. Therefore, let us not forsake our assembly (see Heb 10:25), that is, neglect to participate in the Holy Mass, but rather, "for as often as you shall

74 Ibid.

eat this bread and drink the chalice, you shall shew the death of the Lord, until he come" (1 Cor 11:26).

Lord Jesus, burn the image of your holy face into me
that I may become a revelation of your glory,
that I may proclaim as did the holy Apostle:
"It is no longer I who live, but Christ who lives in me." Amen.

Optional Scripture Readings: Exodus 12:1–13; John 6: 40–59; Mark 14:26; Mark 15:23; 1 Corinthians 11:23–27; Revelation 5:1–12

FULFILL YOUR SELECTED SPIRITUAL PRACTICES FROM STAGE 7: *LOVE AND LEGACY.*

Day 45

(Lent Week 6: Good Friday)

INVOCATION: JESUS, THANK YOU FOR GRANTING ME PARADISE.

THE PROMISE OF PARADISE

Jesus Promises the Good Thief Eternal Beatitude

"Amen I say to thee: this day thou shalt be with
me in paradise." Luke 23:43

Though a person may be tempted to believe that the intense
suffrages endured by Jesus were a series of coincidental
circumstances, after one examines the details of the Passion narrative through the numerous, associated prophetic Old Testament
passages, it is very evident that every detail of Christ's Passion was
willed by God.

One of those divinely ordained details was the context of Christ's
Crucifixion: He was crucified between two sinners (see Lk 23:33).
He was at the center of them. God purposefully and providentially
arranged that Jesus, even while grasping for His last breath, would
have the grace-filled opportunity to save a soul from the clutches
of the devil.

Threaded throughout Jesus' public ministry is His constant, radically intentional desire to endure the ugliest and most shameful situations for the noble purpose of saving just one sinner. Indeed, our Lord's parables of the Two Sons, the Prodigal Son, the Wheat and the Tares, and the Sheep and the Goats—all of which express Jesus' invitation to receive His salvation—are embodied in His final agonizing moments while fixed to the Cross.

In the parable of the Two Sons, a father gives one son a command, to which the elder son initially responds with his yes but lives out his no, while the younger son responds with his no but later responds with his yes.

The parable of the Prodigal Son is the story of two sons. The younger, being rebellious, demands that his portion of the inheritance be given to him. After his father complies, he takes the inheritance and travels to a foreign land, whereupon he squanders it. As he begins to starve, he repents and returns to his father. The other, "obedient" son, who never disobeyed his father, refused to enter the celebration of his rebellious brother's return. The younger son's life is defined ultimately by repentance and filial trust, whereas the older brother's life is—at this point—is defined by moral rigidity and a refusal of God's mercy.

By conveying a visual of the Last Judgement, Jesus depicts Himself as the Just Judge who stands at the center of humanity, who separates the sheep, that is, the penitent who trusts in God mercy and has reformed his life, and the goats, that is, those who either attempt to justify themselves by their own good works or despair of God's mercy for lack of those good works.

These parables all express the truth that Jesus inserts Himself among sinners for the purpose of affording every man the opportunity to either trust in His mercy, believe in His goodness, and demonstrate that belief by participating in a life of good works, or to reject the merciful God and His call to repentance.

Though God's grace is essentially what justifies and sanctifies man, nevertheless, a man must walk in the good works that God has prepared for us to work (see Eph 2:10). Man must participate in his own salvation. As St. Augustine said, "the God who created you without you, will not redeem you without you."[75] Works are necessary, though they are not the source of salvation but the participation and proof of it, for "faith also, if it have not works, is dead in itself" (Jas 2:17; see Jas 2:20). For every man shall be judged according to his works (see Rom 2:6).

When asked what work must be done to inherit eternal life, Jesus responded, "This is the work of God, that you believe in him whom he hath sent" (Jn 6:29). This adequately sums up the Catholic understanding of man's participation in procuring his own salvation: Faith is a *work of God*, awarded to man, by no merit of his own. Yet, man must respond to this unmerited grace by believing in the goodness of God's Son and by repenting of his sinful ways, and, by living a life of charity, he "merits" eternal life that is already merited to him by God. This is the "work of faith" (2 Thes 1:11).

"Protestants often misunderstand the Catholic teaching on merit, thinking that Catholics believe that one must do good works to come to God and be saved. This is exactly the opposite of what the Church teaches. The Council of Trent stressed: "none of those things which preceded justification, whether faith or works, merit the grace of

75 St. Augustine, Sermo 169, 13.

justification, for it is by grace, it is not now by works; otherwise, as the Apostle [Paul] says, grace is no more grace (decree on Justification, 8, citing Rom 11:6)."[76]

Justification, that is, for a sinner to be made just in God's sight, can only be a grace given by God and not by men, lest any man should boast (see Eph 2:9). After God's justification of the sinner, He lavishly bestows grace for the sanctification of man, that he be made holy unto the Lord. Even this is a grace that is not merited by man. Yet, man's participation in the process of sanctification, that is, his response to grace, is meritorious.

"The Catholic Church teaches only Christ is capable of meriting in the strict sense—mere man cannot (see CCC 2007). The most merit humans can have is, when under the influence of God's grace, they perform acts which please Him and which He has promised to reward (see Rom 2:6-11; Gal 6:6-10). Thus, God's grace and his promise form the foundation of all merit."[77]

The drama of salvation, and particularly man's eternal destiny, depends on justification and sanctification—both enacted by God—and on man's participation, which is dependent upon God's grace. Christ deliberately inserts Himself amongst sinners to induce a response from man, either for or against God.

It is interesting to note that both of the criminals crucified on Jesus' right and left reviled Him (see Mt 27:44; Mk 15:32), but, in Luke's Gospel account, a miraculous transformation in one of the thieves transpired.

76 Catholic Answers, https://www.catholic.com/tract/reward-and-merit.
77 Ibid.

Jesus' patient endurance of His unspeakable sufferings, and His last words from the Cross, radiated the unlimited charity of God, and it was this charity that penetrated the broken heart of the good thief. This thief came to recognize that Jesus is a king truly, as revealed by his plea, "Lord, remember me when thou shalt come into thy *kingdom*" (Lk 23:42, emphasis added). We can only deduce that during those bitter hours on the Cross, the good thief witnessed the unimaginable: a man tortured, twisted, and marred beyond recognition, who was verbally and physically accosted, continually while hanging from the tree, yet who exercised complete mastery of himself, never succumbing to vengeance or retaliation but, instead, begged His heavenly Father to forgive His executioners and assailants.

This thief could have been like Judas and succumbed to despairing of God's mercy, but, in a moment of great trust and abandon, he pleaded with Jesus to save him, to draw him to Christ's side in His kingdom, to which "Jesus said to him: Amen I say to thee: This day thou shalt be with me in paradise" (Lk 23:43).

One thief robs himself of his own salvation, while the other, during his last dying moments, steals heaven. The grace of justification and sanctification has been won for both, but only the good thief participated with grace and received the promise of eternal life.

Indeed, "He bestowed forgiveness, the crown He will pay out. Of forgiveness He is the donor; of the crown, He is the debtor. Why debtor? Did He receive something? ... The Lord made Himself a debtor not by receiving something but by promising something. One does not say to Him, 'Pay for what you received,' but 'Pay what you promised.'"[78]

---

78 St. Augustine, *Explanations of the Psalms* 83:12 (AD 405).

Make use then of the brief time you have remaining while living on this earth. Will you respond to the summons to sanctity and participate in the sanctifying grace you have received from God?

Bear in mind, my son, that "according to thy hardness and impenitent heart, thou treasurest up to thyself wrath, against the day of wrath and revelation of the just judgment of God: Who will render to every man according to his works. To them indeed who, according to patience in good work, seek glory and honour and incorruption, eternal life: But to them that are contentious and who obey not the truth but give credit to iniquity, wrath and indignation" (Rom 2:5–8).

"Be penitent, therefore, and be converted, that your sins may be blotted out" (Acts 3:19). By doing so, you will be like the good thief, who, after his death, entered eternal paradise: Christ Himself.

Lord Jesus, burn the image of your holy face into me
that I may become a revelation of your glory,
that I may proclaim as did the holy Apostle:
"It is no longer I who lives but Christ who lives in me." Amen.

———————

Optional Scripture Readings: Luke 15:11–32; Luke 23:32–43;
Matthew 13:24–30; Matthew 21:28–32; Matthew 25:31–46

———————

FULFILL YOUR SELECTED SPIRITUAL PRACTICES FROM STAGE 7:
LOVE AND LEGACY.

+ JMJ +

Day 46

(Lent Week 6: Holy Saturday)

INVOCATION: JESUS, GRANT ME THE GRACE
TO TRUST COMPLETELY GOD THE FATHER.

CHRIST'S GIFT TO HIS FATHER

Jesus Commends His Spirit to God

———

"Father, into thy hands I commend my spirit." Luke 23:46

With complete mastery over His life, amidst His last breath, "Jesus crying with a loud voice, said: Father, into thy hands I commend my spirit. And saying this, he gave up the ghost" (Lk 23:46).

The life of Jesus definitively demonstrates that God's love is self-giving—self-emptying. Christ held back nothing for Himself but rather gave all of Himself to and for mankind's salvation. With utter trust and abandonment, He surrendered His life, His spirit, to His Father. This act is one of complete filial trust. Jesus believed in the goodness of His Father and knew with certainty that His Father had given Him the power to overcome the death that awaited Him.

Jesus's mission was to become man and gather all of humanity into Himself and bring humanity in Himself to His Father. Yet, He must do so by being completely untethered to any human attachment. In the final analysis, Jesus gave away His Body and Blood as food for man; He donated His flesh during the scourging; He surrendered His kingly rights while being crowned with thorns; He relinquished His physical freedom by being nailed to the Cross; He resigned all self-protection by giving away His clothing; He gave His Mother to the beloved disciple; and, ultimately, He gave His spirit to His Father. Christ is the definitive expression of God's identity, which is radical, perpetual, self-giving love.

The pattern of Jesus' mission to save mankind is reflected in the axiom: *exitus, reditus* (exit and return). Jesus exited heaven for the purpose of gathering all men into His assumed humanity, and then He returned to His heavenly Father with all humanity in Him.

Testifying to this reality, Jesus said, "I came forth from the Father and am come into the world: again I leave the world and I go to the Father" (Jn 16:28).

The Passion narrative is bookended by Jesus' complete, radical, abandonment to His father's will that commenced in the Garden of Gethsemane as He prayed, "Not as I will, but as thou wilt" (Mt 26:39), and His last breath as He cried, "Into thy hands I commend my spirit" (Lk 23:46). Jesus' life is one of complete surrender to His Father's will, and, for this reason, His Father is always pleased with Him (see Jn 8:29).

Christ's life is a perfect witness to the unfailing, unfaltering trust in God the Father's mercy: that His Father would not only save Him from the grave but glorify Him before all men.

Jesus last cry, "Into thy hands I commend my spirit" not only expressed His perfect trust in His Father but was a phrase intentionally chosen by Christ as an unmistakable signal, a message of His ultimate victory over and deliverance from evil.

The phrase "into thy hands I commend my spirit" (Ps 31:5) "was the prayer every Jewish mother taught her child to say last thing at night."[79] Therefore, Christ's words would have helped those present at His Crucifixion to recall the entirety of the psalm, which is a prophetic foreshadowing of Christ's Passion and also a prayer of unfailing hope in God amidst His life's destruction, which was being fulfilled before their very eyes.

"I am become a reproach among all my enemies, and very much to my neighbors; and a fear to my acquaintances. They that saw me without fled from me. I am forgotten as one dead from the heart" (Ps 31:11-12). This was fulfilled when Jesus' disciples abandoned Him.

Again, "I am become as a vessel that is destroyed. For I have heard the blame of many that dwell round about. While they assembled together against me, they consulted to take away my life" (Ps 31:12-13). This was fulfilled when the council of the Sanhedrin plotted to kill Jesus by receiving Caiaphas' counsel: "Neither do you consider that it is expedient for you that one man should die for the people and that the whole nation perish not" (Jn 11:50).

Again, "But I have put my trust in thee, O Lord: I said: Thou art my God. My lots are in thy hands (Ps 31:14-15)." "Blessed be the Lord, for he hath shewn his wonderful mercy to me in a fortified city" (Ps 31:21). This represents Christ's confidence in God His Father.

Finally, Jesus prays, "Father, into thy hands I commend my spirit" indicating to all who knew Psalm 31 that the prophecy contained therein had been fulfilled in their presence.

"Christ, makes an act of supreme confidence, throws himself into His Father's arms, and freely gives up His life. He was not

79 Barclay, Commentary Gospel of Luke, 342.

forced to die nor did He die against His will; He died because He wanted to die."[80] This is most evident by the fact that, precisely after Jesus commended His spirit to His Father, He promptly died.

> It was the peculiar privilege of Christ the Lord to have died when He himself decreed to die, and to have died not so much by external violence as by internal ascent. Not only his death, but also its time and place, were ordained by him. For thus Isaiah wrote: He was offered because it was his own will (Isa 53:7). The Lord before his Passion declared the same of himself, "I lay down my life, that I may take it again. No one takes it from me, but I lay it down of my own accord. I have power to lay it down, and I have power to take it again" (Jn 10:17).[81]

The prophetic Messianic psalm ends as if Christ Himself is imploring us: "O love the Lord, all ye his saints: for the Lord will require truth, and will repay them abundantly who act proudly. Do ye manfully, and let your heart be strengthened, all ye that hope in the Lord" (Ps 31:23–24).

My son, Jesus, having justified us before God, now summons you—in the face of great evil and ultimately death—to act manfully and allow God to embolden you in the power of the Lord.

The Church, in her wisdom, daily ends her hours of prayers echoing the last words uttered by Jesus before giving up His spirit: "Into your hands, O lord, I commend my spirit."[82] As Christ ended His days, so we are to end ours, with confident hope in God;

80 *Navarre Bible Commentary*, Luke, 255.
81 St. Pius V, *Catechism* I, 6,7; *Navarre Bible Commentary*, Luke, 255.
82 Liturgy of the Hours, Night Prayer, Responsory.

abandoning our spirit to God our Father, trusting that He will raise our mortal bodies from the grave.

Lord Jesus, burn the image of your holy face into me
that I may become a revelation of your glory,
that I may proclaim as did the holy Apostle:
"It is no longer I who live, but Christ who lives in me." Amen.

Optional Scripture Readings: Psalms 31; John 8:23–29; Luke 23:44–46

FULFILL YOUR SELECTED SPIRITUAL PRACTICES FROM STAGE 7:
LOVE AND LEGACY.

Easter Sunday

You, Come Follow Me

The Resurrection of Jesus Christ

———

"I am the resurrection and the life: he that believeth in me,
although he be dead, shall live." John 11:25

Three days have passed since Holy Thursday night, when after
Jesus had been betrayed and apprehended by the Jewish
authorities, Peter with resolute, stalwart courage, followed his
captured Lord into the high priest's courtyard to witness Jesus' trial
before a partially assembled Sanhedrin.

Within the courtyard, while in close proximity to Jesus, before the
cock crowed twice, Peter denied his affiliation with Christ three times,
as the Lord had foretold. After voicing his third denial, his and the
Savior's eyes met, and, unable to bear the piercing, sorrowful, gaze of
the silent Lamb of God, Peter fled into the night while weeping bitterly.

Over the course of the following three days, Peter's soul endured
severe torment and temptation. Convicted by his lack of fidelity to
Jesus, Peter was hammered by doubt and despair. Peter desperately
desired to see Jesus one last time for the purpose of pleading for
His forgiveness, yet his friend was now dead—and, therefore, also
apparently any hope for reconciliation with Him.

Yet, within Peter remained a faint hope based on Jesus' promise given to him during the Last Supper, "But I have prayed for thee, that thy faith fail not: and thou, being once converted, confirm thy brethren" (Lk 22:32).

Ashamed and heartbroken, Peter, nevertheless, did return to his brethren and the seven of them went fishing. "And they went forth and entered into the ship: and that night they caught nothing" (Jn 21:3).

> But when morning was come, Jesus stood on the shore: yet the disciples knew not that it was Jesus. Jesus therefore said to them: Children have you any meat? They answered him: No. He saith to them: Cast the net on the right side of the ship; and you shall find. They cast therefore: and now they were not able to draw it, for the multitude of fishes. That disciple therefore whom Jesus loved said to Peter: It is the Lord. Simon Peter, when he heard that it was the Lord, girt his coat about him (for he was naked) and cast himself into the sea. (Jn 21:4–7)

Peter most certainly recognized that this miraculous catch of fish was the reenactment of the very moment when Christ first summoned Peter to follow Him (see Lk 5:1–11). It was on that occasion that Jesus preached from Peter's ship to the multitudes on the shoreline and, then, concluding His sermon, commanded Simon Peter to go out into the deep for a catch. Though Simon initially resisted, he nevertheless obeyed and let down his nets and procured a miraculous catch of fish. "When Simon Peter saw, he fell down at Jesus' knees, saying: Depart from me, for I am sinful man, O Lord" (Lk 5:8). Now, after his denial, rather than asking that the Lord depart from him, Peter longed to be forgiven for departing from his Lord.

Peter's nakedness is a symbol of his spiritual shame, which he attempts to cover as he clothes himself before plunging into the sea. Peter swam desperately and with great fervor in hopes that he might have a private moment with Jesus, in hopes of pleading for forgiveness, and to ultimately prove his fidelity to his Lord.

Yet, when he arrived at the shore, the others arrived simultaneously with the fish, and "they saw hot coals lying, and a fish laid thereon, and bread" (Jn 21:9). Jesus asked them to bring some of the catch. Yet, why does He make this request when He already has something to eat? Our Lord does not need Peter's catch, but rather He desires Peter to be caught by His love. Our Lord does not need any of your good works per se but wants *you*, that you may experience His divine love.

A charcoal fire is mentioned only twice in all of Sacred Scripture: The first occasion is during the account of Peter's denial of Christ, and the second occasion is at the appearance of the resurrected Lord on the shore. This charcoal fire, like the catch of the fishes, will be a second opportunity for Peter to respond to Christ's call.

On this beach, amidst the charcoal fire, Jesus asks Peter three times: "Simon, son of John, lovest thou me more than these?" (Jn 21:15). To which Simon responds three time affirmatively, and three times Jesus commissions Peter to feed Christ's sheep. This threefold confession of Peter's love for Christ is Jesus giving Peter the opportunity to repent of his threefold denial.

The first two occasions that Jesus asks Peter if he loves Him, Jesus uses the Greek word *agape,* which is rendered love. To which Peter responds, "Yea, Lord, thou knowest that I love (*philo*) thee" (Jn 21:15). The Greek word rendered love is *philo,* which is a type of brotherly love, whereas *agape* is an unconditional, altruistic, divine love. It is as if Jesus was asking Peter, "If you cannot love Me as I love you can you even love Me as a brother."

The Latin translation is just as revealing. Jesus asked Peter, "Do you love (*diligis*) me. Peter responded by saying "I love (*amo*) you."

Amo is a love of the appetite or passions that is almost casual, an automated response, unregulated by the will; whereas, according to St. Thomas Aquinas and St. Augustine, *diligis* is love that "presupposes and act of election, choice (*electio*). This is why brute animals are not said to love (*diligere*)."[83] To truly love is to *choose* to love with the intellect and will.

Too often, humans initially "love" (*amo*) another with the passions, and, after those passions fade, they lack the will to choose to love (*diligis*) the person. Jesus desired that Peter choose to love his Lord with his whole heart, soul, mind, and strength—with the choice of a determined *agape*. Jesus does not want casual passionate followers but rather those who choose Him above all else. Indeed, Jesus, who initially chose Peter, asked Peter to choose Him. Love is a mutual choosing, a choice to love the other unconditionally, sacrificially, and permanently.

The summons of St. Peter to choose Christ amidst the miracle of the catch of the fish and the charcoal fire is Jesus' way of saying, "Though your love for me failed, my love for you will not fail. Though you have rejected me, I have not rejected you. I have chosen you, and My choice remains."

Between the events of Simon's first calling and this second calling to follow Jesus, was the event of Jesus' Passion and sacrificial death on the Cross. The Cross, standing as a bridge between Peter's

---

83 St. Thomas Aquinas, *Commentary on the Gospel of John*, 506.

initial summons and Christ's second calling of Peter, is a symbol of the irrevocable, permanent election and calling of Christ. Though we may fail Christ, though we may have denied Him, if only we but look to the Cross, repent of our ways, and return to Him, trusting in His infinite mercy, He will reinstate us to our office, to our calling, "for God's gifts and his call are irrevocable" (Rom 11:29, NIV). Look then upon Christ's Cross and draw close and see what thy sins have caused but draw closer and see the love with which they are forgiven.

My son, though you may have fallen from grace and, perhaps, denied our Lord, if you but return to Him, repenting of your sinful ways, trusting in God's unfathomable mercy, surely Jesus will reinstate you to your noble calling. Indeed, Jesus' sacrifice is divine proof that "if we are faithless, he remains faithful, for he cannot disown himself" (2 Tm 2:13, NIV).

Therefore, let us not remain faithless, but appeal to our Lord's mercy with the faith of Christ, for He says, "You have not chosen me: but I have chosen you; and have appointed you, that you should go, and should bring forth fruit; and your fruit should remain" (Jn 15:16). Though you, like St. Peter, may have for a moment lost your way, nevertheless, "Follow thou me" (Jn 21:22).

+ JMJ +

Consecration to Jesus Christ, Son of God the Father

"This salutary reparation to the Holy Face of Jesus is a Divine Work, destined to save modern society." Pope Bl. Pius IX

Lord Jesus Christ, the only begotten Son of God, the Eternal Word who deemed not equality with God something to be clung to but rather, by the Holy Spirit, emptied Thyself and became incarnate, permanently uniting Thy divinity to human nature that in Thee, human nature may be united eternally to God.

Submitting to Thy Father's Holy Will, Thou became obedient unto death, even death on a Cross. Thou drank from the stream by the wayside and have lifted Thy head in triumph; therefore, God has highly exalted Thee, imparting to Thee the name that ranks above all names, and it is to this Holy Name that I now, in the presence of the heavenly host, to the honor of God the Father, bend my knees.

Thou are the Lamb of God, once slain, yet who lives forever. Thou conquered sin and death in Thy body, and, for all eternity, Thou present Thy sacrificed, yet glorified, flesh before the Father, that for eternity all flesh, including myself, may partake in Thy divine nature. You alone are worthy to receive power, divinity, wisdom, strength, honour, glory, and benediction.

Yet, in sin was I conceived and habitually have I conceived sin. Rebellious and defiant, I have disobeyed Thy precepts; despicable and pathetic, I am burdened under the heavy load of my transgressions; weak in faith, I have doubted Thy eternal goodness; lacking in hope, I have wallowed in discouragement; and slow to charity, I have slipped into indifference.

Like the unforgiving steward whose massive debt was beyond comprehension and restitution, if I could live a thousand lifetimes with every moment and breath dedicated to Thy holy service, impossible would it be to make recompense for even the smallest portion of my heinous crimes against Thy Divine Majesty.

It is beyond my power and capacity to live a single day without adding to my debt, for so says the sacred text: the just man doth fall seven times a day (see Prv 24:6).

Furthermore, beyond not being capable of paying the debt of my sin, I am unable to contribute anything of value or worth that would compensate for Thy lavish benevolence, who has given me honor, glory, and power, placing all things under my feet.

The power to justify myself in Thy sight is beyond me, and, without Thy divine predilection, I am doomed to eternal perdition.

Therefore, this day, in the presence of the host of angels, especially my guardian angel, the most holy Apostles, the virgins and martyrs, and, most especially, my parents in the order of grace—Mary, my Mother most holy, and St. Joseph, her most chaste spouse—I surrender myself, all that I am, and all that I possess, that I may be possessed by Thee and Thy Divine Will.

Far too long have I thought with the mind of the world. I now intend, with the firmest resolution, to put off the old man and think only with the divine mind of the New and Everlasting Man, Jesus

Christ. It is not enough that I be justified in Thy sight. Sanctify me by living in me, that I may forever live in Thee.

Blessed are Thou, Hosanna in the Highest! The doors of my heart grow higher, that Thou may enter O King of glory. Do Thou enter me, Thy temple, which I have allowed to become a haunt of demons, a den of thieves, and a house of idolatry. Drive out all that is evil from me and sweep clean this house. Enthrone Thyself upon my most wretched, calloused, and needful heart that I may become a living manifestation and revelation of Thy divine presence, that I may truly proclaim with the holy Apostle that it is no longer I who live, but Thou, O Christ, who lives in me. Come then, Divine Savior, and sanctify this house; burn Thy Holy Image into me that I may be a living representation of Your Divine Love, for without Thee I can do nothing.

Thou, who are the Way, the Truth, and the Life, show me Thy Way and give me the grace to walk in Thy Truth that I may live Thy Life, and Thy Life may be lived in me. Indeed, Thou in me, and I in Thee, may the Son of God live in me that I may live in the God the Son eternally.

Grace me, O Holy Spirit, that I may be a true and faithful son of God our Father, a lamb of the Lamb of God, a living sacrifice of praise.

O my God, who possessed no body, yet assumed a body forever, and suffered and sacrificed Thyself in that body, animate me that I, too, may glorify God in my body, that I may become a holy and living sacrifice unto God Almighty, that this may be my spiritual worship, and that God who has begun this good work in me will see it unto completion.

For holocausts and offerings Thou does not desire, instead here am I, a body Thou hast prepared for me.

Therefore having the mind of Him who sanctifies those who are sanctified, I consecrate myself entirely, all that I possess spiritually and temporally, without reserve, to Thee O Jesus Christ, offering myself to Thee that through Thee, with Thee, and in Thee, Thou would consecrate me to God the almighty Father, that He may see fit to do with me as He desires for His good pleasure and for His greater glory in time and in eternity.

What thanks shall I render the Lord for the good He has done unto me? I shall raise the chalice of salvation and call upon the name of the Lord. May I be lifted up in the One who, by being lifted up in sacrifice, has drawn all men to Himself.

May the life that Thou has so generously entrusted to me be lived and given for the threefold purpose of the glory of God, the salvation of souls, and eternal communion with the Triune God for all eternity. Amen.

+ JMJ +

Spiritual Practices

STAGE 1 SPIRITUAL PRACTICES

1. THE HOLY FACE DAILY DEVOTION

Throughout the centuries the reverent devotion to the Holy Face of Jesus has flourished, particularly gaining more notoriety through St. Thérèse of Lisieux, who took the religious name "St. Thérèse of the Child Jesus and of the Holy Face." After being canonized and proclaimed Doctor of the Church, her devotion, prayers, and practices concerning the Holy Face of Jesus have become widely known. The earnest desire of the believer, like St. Thérèse, is to resemble and reflect the person of Jesus to those that they encounter that they may encounter Christ. For this purpose we tape the image of the Holy Face of Jesus (included in this book on page 301) to a mirror upon which we normally look at ourselves as we prepare for our day. Each day, many times a day, we look upon this image of Jesus's Holy Face, rather than our own face, praying, *"Lord Jesus, burn the image of your holy face into me that I may become a revelation of your glory; that I may proclaim as did the holy apostle, "It is no longer I who lives but Christ who lives in me. Amen."* Daily we practice this devotion with the sincere hope that we may become an *Alter Christus*, another Christ, for that is the purpose of our consecration: to become a son of God in God the Son, that we may become spiritual fathers who reflect and reveal God the Father.

STAGE 2 SPIRITUAL PRACTICES

2. DAILY MORNING OFFERING

Upon waking, prior to viewing any emails or texts—or doing anything else—drop down to the floor and surrender yourself, and your day, to God. By previewing or viewing texts or emails, listening to podcasts, music, or the news prior to your morning offering, you will have surrendered to the world instead of giving your first fruits to God. In addition, when possible, make your morning offering on your knees and with your head bowed down to the floor. The reason for this is that your body expresses what your soul believes. By kneeling, or praying in a prostrate position, your body express that you are spiritually submitting and surrendering your soul to God's Holy Will. Your morning offering consists of offering to God the Father all that you are and have, through, with, and in His Son, Jesus Christ; imploring the Holy Spirit to animate and direct you throughout the day; and offering yourself to Jesus Christ in the manner by which He came to us: through the union of the Virgin Mary and St. Joseph. The purpose behind your morning offering is simply "reporting for duty," acknowledging to God your worship of Him and your readiness to serve Him wholeheartedly.

Sample morning offering: Heavenly Father, I offer you my day; all that I am and have to you—spiritual, temporal, physical, thoughts, memory, will, and good actions—through, with, and in your Son, our Lord, Jesus Christ, in union with all the Masses offered throughout the world, for the conversion of sinners, for the reparation of sins, for the holy souls in purgatory to be drawn into your Divine Light, and most of all, for the love of Thee, My God. Lord Jesus. I do not presume to come to you alone; but rather approach you in the way You came to us, through the holy union of the Blessed Virgin and St. Joseph, her chaste spouse. Holy Mary, good St. Joseph, by your union of wills and your intercession before God, obtain for me the gift of the Holy Spirit, that our Lord Jesus may be conceived ever anew in me.

3. DAILY MORNING PRAYER

(15 minutes/including 5 minutes of silence)
Secularists have been known to say, "Win the morning, win the day." The truth of this idea is born from the Christian ideal, particularly the monastic life, wherein the man who seeks God first is blessed in his work, efforts, and initiatives. Indeed, the Christian who gives God his morning's first moments will be given God's presence throughout his day. There exist many methods and forms of prayer that are far too numerous to mention here. The main purpose of your morning prayer is to allow yourself the time

and space to cultivate a relationship with God and be drawn into His Trinitarian communion of Persons. Morning prayer is different than the morning offering: the morning offering is reporting for duty and asking God's blessing on one's day; the morning prayer is to be with and rest with God. Morning prayer consists of worship and praise, divine revelation as the source of conversation with God, and petition. To cultivate this divine conversation, a primer is very helpful, such as the Liturgy of the Hours, Sacred Scripture, or a reflection from a reliable devotional. The Liturgy of the Hours is an excellent resource that helps you "converse" with God by using preset psalms, prayers, and petitions that are segmented by the time, or "hours," of the day: Lauds is the morning prayer of the Church. Regardless of what source you use as the "launching pad" for your prayer with God, we must remember that these things are not "prayer" itself, but the "gas" that is poured on the hot coals of God's presence within the soul. The Holy Spirit then fans these embers into flame. After you have conversed with God, spend several minutes in silence, waiting upon Him. This time is essential to allowing God the time and space to speak or infuse Himself into your soul. After this period of silence, offer your petitions and thanksgiving to Him; and if possible, make a resolution that you will carry out throughout your day. End your prayer with a Glory Be.

4. DAILY ROSARY

The Rosary is the chain that binds Satan. The Rosary is not a mere repetition of idle words, but a devotion to Our Blessed Mother, who leads us in meditation on Christ's life. Indeed, by "holding her hand," we see Jesus and His life through her eyes; and feeling with her heart, she helps to unlock the sacred mysteries of Christ's life, from His Incarnation through His Ascension, and the outpouring of His Holy Spirit on the Church. There exists a grave temptation or at least a tendency to rush through the prayers of the Rosary, rattling them off like an auctioneer; or to zone out and think of other things while saying the words. Due to the repetitive nature of the prayer, it is easy to understand how these things happen. To overcome such temptations, remember that the quality of prayer is more important than the quantity of words. The Rosary is a journey with Mary, following Christ and learning to be His disciple. Considering this, it can be highly beneficial to begin praying the

Rosary by praying only one or two decades or by using a Scriptural Rosary. A Scriptural Rosary allows one to enter more deeply into the mystery being meditated upon by reciting a brief scriptural passage for each bead prior to praying the Hail Mary. For example, if you are praying the First Sorrowful Mystery, before saying the first Hail Mary, recite the verse: "Jesus took His disciples to the garden of Gethsemane and asked them to watch and pray." Prior to the second Hail Mary, you may recite the next verse: "Jesus said to His disciples, 'Pray that you may not fall into temptation.'" Prior to the third Hail Mary, "For the spirit is willing, but the flesh is weak," and so on. By praying the Rosary this way, you will be able to penetrate more deeply into the sacred mysteries of Christ, and thus His prayer can be more meaningful and profitable.

5. Scripture meditation: The Seven R's of Prayer

There is a way to transform our prayer from a monologue to a dialogue; from a relationship to a "real-ationship;" from being filled with words to making us capable of discerning and receiving the true Word. This way is the seven Rs of prayer. The seven Rs is an outline for prayer that if used daily will open you to God who will transform you into a father of glory.

Recognize God's Presence

The steps to effective prayer are, first, *recognize* God's presence *in you*. Often we begin prayer, launching into what we want to say, directing our thoughts to the God who seems to be somewhere "out there." Pause and greet God who lives within you. This can be done by making the sign of the cross devoutly and slowly, bowing your head, or simply saying, "Hello, God, I'm here. Hello, God, you are here." But most importantly, we ought to pause for a moment of silence reverently acknowledging that we are humbly placing ourselves in the presence of God who has placed His presence within us.

Read God's Word

Second, every conversation has a context, a topic for discussion. It is no different with our relationship with God. Considering this, the second R of prayer is *read*. It is important to read God's Word, particularly the Gospel, which contextualizes our prayer. We read until something strikes us, or a phrase connects with us. Perhaps we reread the same passage a couple of times.

Reflect on a Word or Phrase

Third, after you have identified a phrase or a word that God is using to speak to you, *reflect* on that word or phrase. Meditate and consider what God is trying to communicate to you through His word.

Respond to God

Fourth, after reflecting, we *respond* to God. We do this by discussing our dreams, aspirations, desires, struggles, plans for the day, our sins, fears, and anxieties—we simply tell Him all about it. During this time we ask for His help and guidance, and for Him to grant success to the work of our hands (see Psalm 90).

Rest in God

The fifth R is *rest*. After you have recognized God's presence, read His Word, reflected on the phrase that resonates with you, and responded to His Word, then it is time to rest in Him. Simply remain in His presence silently for several minutes. This, perhaps, is the most essential aspect of prayer. During this time of rest God infuses His very presence and life into us.

Make a Resolution

Sixth, after you have rested in God, then make a *resolution* in the form of a request: God please help me do this today.

Remember Your Resolution

The seventh R is to *remember* your resolution throughout the day, returning to the divine guidance that you received during prayer.

By humbly entering the silence daily and listening in this manner, you can be certain that God will transform your life. You will become a father of purpose, peace, power, and passion, who is capable of transmitting God's love and mercy to his family.

STAGE 3 SPIRITUAL PRACTICES

6. DAILY EXAMINATION OF CONSCIENCE

Toward the end of day, prior to retiring for the evening or before getting into bed, take a couple of moments to examine your conscience. To do this, assume a prayerful position such as kneeling or lying prostrate, and invoke the Holy Spirit to help you examine your thoughts, words, and actions during the day. This does not need to be an exacting process. Ideally, first recount the blessings of the day and gives God thanks for them. Second, reflect upon and confess to God those of your actions, thoughts, and words that were not in conformity with God's holy will or are sinful. Third, after confessing your sins, make a heartfelt act of contrition, asking God for His mercy, forgiveness, and the grace necessary to avoid the near occasion of sin in the future. The Ten Commandments can be used as a guide by which you can examine your conscience, but sometimes these commandments may be too broad and general. Another powerful way to examine yourself is by using Christ's Beatitudes. For example:

Blessed are the poor in Spirit . . . Was I prideful, self-seeking, self-glorifying, self-important, placing myself above others today? Have I responded to the people and circumstances in my life with humility, accepting them as though they are from God?

Blessed are the meek . . . Did I allow anger to be the driving force behind my actions? Did I vent my anger, raise my voice, and act in a demeaning way to those around me? Do I allow Church politics, government politics, family situations, obstacles at work or at home to arouse my anger? Or do I give such situations to God and allow the Holy Spirit to help me deal with them rationally and calmly?

Blessed are those who mourn . . . Do I have true sorrow and contrition for my sins? Have I repented and done penance for my past sins? Do I seriously consider that my sins of the past may have led individuals to sin against God, perhaps even damnation? Do I ask God to make right my wrongs and redeem my omissions? Do I consider that it was for my sins that the Son of God was tortured and gave His life?

Blessed are those who hunger and thirst for righteousness . . . Do I desire the right over the wrong, the moral over the immoral? Do I rejoice when evil or immorality is lauded? Do I approve of videos, movies, posts, and tweets that contain illicit or immoral messages? Do I share such things, or find humor in them? Am I fair in my dealings with others, particularly in business and finances? Have I stolen anyone's goods, content, or good reputation? If so, have I made amends? Justice is seeking God first and giving Him His due: Do I seek God first in all matters? Do I give God the first fruits of my money and time?

Blessed are the merciful . . . Have I withheld forgiving someone who has offended me? Have I sought forgiveness from someone I have offended or sinned against? Have I judged, condemned, or criticized another unjustly? Have I judged another without considering my own wretchedness, failings, and sins?

Blessed are the pure of heart . . . Do I view the human body as an object of desire, to be used for my disordered gratification? Do I use pornography in any form? Do I avoid or do I submit to the temptation to click on ads, posts, or news feeds that display people in sexually provocative situations? Do I make every attempt to see a woman as an equal, with equal dignity, or do I reduce her to her bodily attributes? Do I use or manipulate people to obtain what I desire from them? Or do I love my neighbor for who they are, without expecting anything in return? Have I been jealous or envious of another's status, talents, gifts, or possessions? Do I praise God for His glory in others, even when I don't possess that particular glory?

7. EVENING PRAYER

It has been said that how we finish our day is how we will finish our life. If we finish our day faithful in prayer and devotion, most likely we will complete our days devoted, faithful, and prayerful. The purpose of evening prayer is to offer worship to God and to cultivate conversation with God. As with morning prayer, to assist in fostering this conversation a primer such as the Liturgy of the Hours, Sacred Scripture, or a reflection from a reliable devotional is very helpful. As we've said, the Liturgy of the Hours helps you converse with God by using preset psalms, prayers, and petitions that are segmented by the time, or "hours," of the day. Vespers is the evening prayer of the Church. Prior to beginning evening prayer, spend a couple of moments in the presence of God, thanking Him for the blessings of the day and examining your conscience. After your examination of conscience, spend some time with God using Sacred Scripture, the Liturgy of the Hours, or a reflection. After you have conversed with God, spend several minutes in silence, waiting upon Him, again to allow God the time and space to speak or infuse Himself into your soul. An important note: we are often tempted to wind down by spending time on social media prior to sleep. Without realizing it, we are giving Satan a foothold in our spiritual life. After your evening prayer, avoid all social media and surrender your sleep to God.

8. SPIRITUAL READING

While it is true that knowledge puffs up, but love builds up (Cf 1 Cor 8:1), to love another presupposes that one knows another. If we are to love Jesus and His Father, it is imperative that we know Christ; for to know Christ is to know His Father. For, "how then shall they call on him, in whom they have not believed? Or how shall they believe him, of who they have not heard? And how shall they hear, without a preacher?" (Rom 10:14). Daily reading of Sacred Scripture, the writings of the saints, or of literary works that convey the goodness and truth of Christ and the Catholic faith, are essential to our relationship with Jesus being further forged and deepened. Indeed, when one does not practice spiritual reading, the mind becomes void of religious thought, and consequently devotion becomes weakened. Where there is a void, something else will fill that space. If we lack attention upon spiritual matters, temporal matters will occupy and enslave our thoughts. The apostle tells us that we are to seek the things above, where Christ is; to set our minds on the things above not earthly things (Cf Col 3:1–2). By daily spiritual reading we are seeking the things above; we are imparted spiritual insights that invite us to meditate on Jesus' life and His teachings, which help to condition our behavior throughout the day. To practically apply the practice of daily spiritual reading, first identify a resource; second, allocate at least ten minutes a day to reading from that source; third, as you read, consider what God is teaching or asking of you. This is how divine intimacy begins and conversation with God begins. For to know God well is complete justice, and to know his might is the root of immortality (Cf Wis 15:1,3).

9. WEEKLY CONFESSION

During our Lenten journey with Jesus, particularly by meditating upon his life and fulfilling our spiritual practices, we become keenly aware of our pathetic spiritual condition. As God exposes to us the foul and festering sickness of sin metastasizing within us, it is imperative that we not suppress, or neglect the spiritual illness, but turn to the divine physician and confess those sinful tendencies, dispositions, and evil actions in an honest and self-condemning way.

To confess one's sins aloud to a priest has both spiritual and practical benefits. When one submits himself to the priest who is in *Persona Christi* he is humbling himself before the very authority that God has established. Further, when a penitent confesses his sins aloud to a priest, it allows him to hear more acutely the despicable and grave character of his offenses, which prompts him to never commit that sin again. The Lord Jesus graces such humility, for as the psalmist says, "A sacrifice to God is an afflicted spirit: a contrite and humble heart, O God, thou wilt not despise" (Ps 51:17). As with all of the sacraments, in the sacrament of confession, the grace obtained by Christ's sacrifice flows from Calvary to the penitent. This is not merely a human act, but rather, a gift of grace afforded by God to the sinner. Sin figuratively plows a furrow in the soul of man, thus leaving a vacuum for Satan to enter and subdue, making it a type of Gehenna, a trash dump of evil. Yet, by confessing one's sins sacramentally, the sinner gives God access to his field–his ouls–granting Him permission to expel the devil and fill that furrow with fresh dirt and new seed–a symbol of grace–which eventually grows and bears new fruit. By means of weekly self-examination, a man becomes sensitive to sinful inclinations. He becomes equipped by God's grace to withstand temptation, conquer evil and thwart the devil's efforts to lodge his vices in a man's soul.

STAGE 4 SPIRITUAL PRACTICES

10. ONE DAILY HIDDEN SIGNIFICANT SACRIFICE

It has been said that prayer without sacrifice is lip service, and sacrifice without prayer is a form of bodily training and self-mastery. Prayer inspires one to sacrifice; and sacrifice inspires the power of prayer. As priest of your domestic church, it is vital that you not only pray, but also sacrifice for your family's sanctity daily. If your sacrifice is to be efficacious, that is, able to transmit grace, it must have the character of secrecy, of being hidden. "Do not let your right hand know what your left hand is doing . . ." The Pharisees were said to blow a horn as they made a monetary donation, and Christ, speaking of them, said that they received their reward. Our sacrifice, therefore, is to be hidden; you are to perform the action without discussing or bringing attention to it; for by drawing attention to yourself, you have negated the power of the offering. A man who sacrifices does so in the image and in imitation of the Heavenly Father who "is in secret" (Mt 6:6). If our fatherhood is to reflect and relive the fatherhood of God, we are to carry out our sacrifices in a hidden way. Be not worried or concerned that you will not be rewarded. Glorify yourself and you will receive that reward. Glorify God and He cannot help but to glorify you; and this glory far surpasses any glory we can give ourselves. In addition to the sacrifice being secret, it ought to be significant; that is, your offering should cost you something. By setting aside that something you desire, are attached to, or have come to depend upon, and giving it to God as an offering, it becomes "holy," set apart, that God may use it to confer grace on you, your family, and humanity in the manner He sees fit. Suggested sacrifices that are significant to the average man are: sleeping on the floor; not using a pillow while you sleep; rising an hour early for prayer; committing to waking when the alarm rings without delay; taking a cold shower; skipping a meal(s); drinking nothing other than water; abstaining from alcohol; abstaining from sexual relations with your wife for a period of time; abstaining from the use of social media; donating money that you want to use for your own desires to a good cause; adoring the Blessed Sacrament several times a week, etc. The key is that the sacrifice be daily; that the motive is for God and the conversion of your family, Christian brothers, neighbors, and their families; that it is accomplished with the motivation of love and not necessarily "self-help" (for example: to lose weight); and that the sacrifice be hidden, as much as possible.

11. REDUCE FORMS OF MEDIA SUCH AS RADIO, MUSIC, NEWS, AND VIDEOS

To become capable of discerning the still, small, interior voice of God, it is vital that the voices of the world be muted. Without this first step, it will be gravely difficult to discern God's mission, vision, and plan for your life. A first step to becoming a man of silence who is capable of receiving God's impulses and divine inspirations is to silence the radio, music, news, and social media feeds while driving in the car or commuting. By doing so, your drive time can become prayer time—a very natural form of meditating—wherein you invite God into the areas of your life where you need divine guidance. Though at first it may feel awkward to be in silence, eventually your soul will crave such moments of solitude and eventually you will begin to notice that God is shaping your conscience and your motivations. Indeed, you will notice the effect of God's presence in your life.

12. NO PHONE, COMPUTER, INTERNET, EMAIL, TEXTING PRIOR TO MORNING PRAYER, OR AFTER EVENING PRAYER

The Lord Jesus invites us to seek first the kingdom of God, promising that all things will be granted to us (Mt 6:33). Too often, however, due to the heavy demands and obligations of our state in life, we feel pressured to hearken to email, text correspondence, or listen and watch news sources to inform ourselves of current events. By doing so, our behavior subconsciously conveys that we depend upon the voices of the world, and the world's gospel more than God, Christ, and His Gospel; or that we deem the creature of greater priority than the Creator. To be effective disciples of Christ, animated by His truth, it is imperative that we seek Jesus' counsel prior to all other voices and demands; and to seek His counsel last, prior to our sleep. By applying ourselves to this daily practice, we give God our first fruits. God, however, will not be outdone in generosity and will give us far more than we can ever give Him. Morning prayer and evening prayer, beginning and ending our day with God our Father, helps us to build our day around God, rather than God around our day, while also helping us to become available to the inspiration of the Holy Spirit who wills to grant success to the work of our hands (Cf Ps 90).

Stage 5 Spiritual Practices

13. One Holy Hour a week

Once per week, make a visit to a chapel that has perpetual Eucharistic Adoration. Make it a point to find a local parish and spend time before our Lord's Eucharistic Presence in the tabernacle. Unfortunately, in modern times, Catholic churches are locked, and for good reasons. Yet we must make every effort to either contact the pastor of a parish, obtain a key, or request entrance to the church for a time of prayer. There is nearly nothing as life-changing and transforming as spending time with Christ in Adoration. You cannot give what you do not possess. To give God you must have God; and to have God you must spend time with God; and one of the most powerful ways to spend time with God is in Eucharistic Adoration. By adoring the Lord in His littleness, silence, and hiddenness, you will be given the power to rejoice and be effective in the little, silent, hidden character of your fatherhood. God cannot be outdone in His generosity. Ultimately, it would be ideal to visit our Lord in the Most Blessed Sacrament daily. Regardless, by giving an hour to our Lord once per week, He will grant you incalculable blessings.

14. Attend one extra Holy Mass per week (in addition to Sunday)

Though the Holy Sacrifice of Jesus Christ is re-presented at every Holy Mass, often–especially at Sunday Mass–we are not fully present. Factors such as attempting to gather the family and arrive at the local parish church prior to the Sacred Liturgy; music that is intended to attract the worshiper to God, by means of its constant clamor, can become a detraction from meditative, discursive prayer; lacking ample time for silence, prayer and preparation prior to receiving our Lord's Body and Blood; distractions during the Mass, all bite at and diminish our ability to give full attention to the Sacred Word and the Sacred Sacrifice. Often, we leave Holy Mass feeling as though we have not entered into the Sacred Mysteries or sensing that those mysteries have entered into us. Weekly daily Mass, by means of its humble simplicity offers a silent, meditative context that affords the worshipper true intimacy and peace with our Lord. Lacking entrance and closing hymns, songs during holy communion, and larger crowds, silence is a key attribute of daily

Mass that enables one to be more attentive to the Sacred Word and respond to that Word intentionally. Additionally, Jesus offers Himself as food that grants spiritual strength, imparting wisdom, guidance, and perseverance during the work week. By receiving our Lord Jesus in the most Blessed Sacrament more frequently, Jesus becomes an accountability partner that prompts a man to live a holy, chaste life. For if he is to receive our Lord he must be in the state of grace. Silent intimacy, strength and spiritual sustenance and accountability with Jesus–all offered in the context of daily Mass–help to fuel the fire of divine love within the soul of the believer thoughout the week.

15. PERSONAL LITANY OF THANKSGIVING

Man, desirous of making peace with God, and demonstrating his affection and love for God, often sets himself to the task of offering tremendous sacrifices to the Lord. At times this may be beneficial, particularly for his own purification and detachment from creatures. However, God, through the psalmist, discloses that the type of sacrifice He desires from men is the sacrifice of thanksgiving, or praise (Cf Ps 50). Sacrifice of this kind demonstrates that one is humble enough to acknowledge that all he has received is a gift from God, and not of his own doing. "What hast thou that hast not received? And if thou hast received, why does thou glory, as if thou hadst not received it?" (1 Cor 4:7). "Every best gift, and every perfect gift, is from above, coming down from the Father of lights" (Jms 1:17). When one reflects upon his life, and the gifts that he has received, he cannot help but to appreciate God's generosity and benevolence. This understanding of God's goodness inspires him to thank God for those gifts received, particularly for God Himself and having a relationship with Him. This spirit of thanksgiving affords joy to the soul and grants a man true delight in God. The psalmist promises: "Delight in the Lord, and he will give thee the requests of thy heart" (Ps 37:4). By giving God thanks, we begin to delight in God, and by delighting in God, God lavishly grants us more of His generosity. Therefore, it is highly beneficial to develop a personal litany of thanksgiving to be recited in the presence of our Eucharistic Lord. When compiling your list, remember to mention not only temporal gifts, such as your health, financial provision, security, lodging and sustenance; but also the spiritual gifts, such as faith, the divine life that flows through the sacraments, God Himself and His goodness; and also the sufferings and plights through which, by God's grace, you have persevered and grown in your capacity to love. Thanksgiving for God and His gifts, breeds joy, joy breeds delight in God, and delight in God draws down more gifts from God above. Therefore, daily we bring before God our litany of thanksgiving for this is the sacrifice that He desires from us.

STAGE 6 SPIRITUAL PRACTICES

16. ONE LARGER CHARITABLE DONATION TO A MISSION OR INSTITUTION THAT WORKS WITH THE LESS FORTUNATE

Though weekly tithing from our gross income is essential, it can become rote and systematic, lacking a certain spirit of charity and compassion. To awaken within us the Lord's love for the poor, during our forty-six-day consecration, we commit ourselves to making a larger contribution to the less fortunate. To give beyond the amount of our typical weekly tithe can instill fear or anxiety. This pain, however, enables us to experience a very small taste of what Christ in His poor feels daily. Giving alms to those in need not only affords a certain detachment from depending upon money for security, but the act of such self-giving renders a person purer. "For we brought nothing into the world; and certainly we can take nothing out" (1 Tim 6:7). Christ has disclosed those things for which we will be judged, and a majority of these involve the helping of the less fortunate (Cf Mt 25). Therefore, "Give alms, and behold; all things are clean to you." (Lk 11:41).

16. VISIT AN ELDERLY, SICK, OR HOMEBOUND PERSON

After the Lord gave the parable of the Good Samaritan, He asked the lawyer who tested Him, "Which of these three, in thy opinion, was neighbor to him that fell among the robbers? But [the lawyer] said: He that showed mercy to him. And Jesus said to him: Go and do thou in like manner" (Lk 10:36–37). To be a true neighbor is to show mercy. So closely does Jesus associate Himself with the poor and less fortunate that He says, "When I was naked you covered *me*; sick and you visited *me*; I was prison, and you came to *me*" (Mt 25:36). Again, Jesus says, "Amen I say to you, as Long as you did it to one of these my least brethren, you did it to *me*" (Mt 25:40). As we age our value –by society's standards– greatly diminishes, and often, we become an afterthought in the minds of those who loved us. The sick, the elderly, particularly those "imprisoned" in nursing homes are the "Me" that Jesus refers to. If we desire to not only be the face of Christ to others, but also see the face of Christ in others, it is imperative that we visit the "imprisoned," the elderly, or family members who we have not seen for some time; spend time with those who sense their inability to contribute, the sick who are often alone and feel so helpless. We may not be capable of providing a remedy for their situation; however, we can provide hope, and that hope enables the lonely person to know the God has not abandoned them.

17. DEVOTE TIME TO ASSISTING SOMEONE WITH A PROJECT

Man can only discover himself by becoming a sincere gift (Cf GS 24). To become who God has created you to be, it is imperative that you give yourself in donation to others. By offering your time and your talents in service to others, you not only help others, but come to know more of yourself and your capabilities. Indeed, by helping another as though they are Christ, you discover Christ within yourself. Truly, this is why it is better to give than to receive; for in giving the Lord's charity to others we discover more of that divine charity living within ourselves. During this forty-six-day consecration, identify a loved one, a shut-in, or someone from your parish who needs help with a project. It could be as simple as raking leaves, removing snow, or more intense like re-wiring electrical, or installing a garbage disposal. If you are unable to identify someone among your family members or neighbors who needs help with a project, ask your parish priest if he is aware of a member from your parish who has a particular need. To offer your services to another can be risky and instill the fear of not being able to help. However, if we allow that fear to incapacitate our ability to offer ourselves in service, another may never experience the benevolence of Christ–which is the goal of assisting others with their project needs.

18. Tithe regularly/give to the poor

One the most effective ways that a child learns to be generous is witnessing his father giving generously to those in need. Sometimes, a dad will give his child the money to put in the collection basket at Mass, or have his child give money or food to a homeless person, in order to involve his child in this act of generosity. This almost always grants divine consolation and inculcates a love for the less fortunate. A generous father teaches his child that God the Father is generous. Indeed, if you as a human father help the poor, your child, who perhaps feels poor in spirit, will trust that God is generous and will provide. To be intentional in this area, keep extra cash on hand, so that if the occasion in which you are asked for help arises, you can provide. Archbishop Fulton Sheen, when asked, after giving money to beggars, why he did so when he knew they would probably misuse the money, responded, "Because I do not know which one is Jesus." A child will see Christ in his father who sees Christ in the poor. When tithing, we give from our total income, that is we give 10% of our gross, or total income. This demonstrates that we belief that all we have been given is from the Lord and for the Lord. God will never be outdone in generosity.

Stage 7 Spiritual Practices

19. Forgive, bless, and intentionally pray for an enemy, someone who has wounded us, or someone you dislike

Forgiveness is the core of the Gospel, it is the pinnacle expression of mercy, and according to Jesus, to forgive one's enemy is to be perfect as God our Father is perfect (Cf Mt 5). While enduring the utmost torment and amidst the most horrific agony, Jesus pleaded that His Father forgive those who had executed Him. This is perfection. St. Paul tells us that we are to forgive others as we have been forgiven by God in Christ (Cf Eph 4:32), which is an immeasurable amount. If we refuse to forgive, however, the condemnation that we impart to others becomes our own condemnation. As Christians we pray and ask Our Father in Heaven to forgive us as we forgive those who trespass against us or are indebted to us. The implication is that the manner by which we forgive, and the degree to which we forgive, will be imparted by God unto us. Jesus says as much: to the measure that you measure, it will be measured out to you (Cf Mt 7:2). There is perhaps no more important action, nor any attribute more Christian, than to forgive in the name of Jesus Christ. It is impossible to live a life without being betrayed by someone who was considered trustworthy, to be wounded by someone whom we loved, to be damaged by an enemy, or simply to be in the presence of someone disagreeable or unlikable. As terrible as another's sin may be, our lack of forgiveness may allow their sin to be the cause of our damnation. During our consecration period, we ask God to reveal to us those persons that we resent, dislike and have not forgiven. After identifying these people, we ask God daily to forgive them, bless them, and grant them His salvation. Only then can we experience the freedom for which Christ has set us free (Cf Gal 5:1).

20. Ask Forgiveness for a Wrong Committed

The soul and the body are inextricably linked. The two, from the beginning, God created to be one–the entire human nature. Though we may sin in the body, it is the soul that directs those misguided actions. Though the soul contains the body, the body contains the stress and duress of unconfessed and unforgiven sins. Mental illness such as chronic depression and anxiety may result from suppressing the sins, and the deplorable acts that one has never sought forgiveness for. We are keenly aware of those people whom we have wronged, wounded, and injured. Our soul will never be at peace until we have sought forgiveness for our offenses from the ones whom we have offended. During this consecration period, we commit ourselves to seek forgiveness, either in person, by phone, or by letter, from someone whom we have injured, offended, wounded, or betrayed. King David, after committing adultery with Bathsheba and having her husband, Uriah, murdered, repented, praying, "The sacrifice to God is an afflicted spirit: a contrite and humbled heart, O God, thou wilt not despise" (Ps 51:17). Humility is the foundation of all of the virtues, without which a man cannot be holy. *Humilitas est veritas*, humility is truth, and to be honest is to be humble enough to admit our wrong and seek forgiveness from the one we have wronged. When you seek forgiveness, do not expect anything from the person whom you are seeking forgiveness from. In fact, they may reject your request. Regardless of the response you receive, the humility in seeking forgiveness affords great freedom. Also, refrain from saying "I'm sorry"; for by doing so, you are simply stating how you feel and consequently decrease your vulnerability. Rather, ask, "will you forgive me?" By asking for forgiveness in this way, you surrender control of your situation to the other, and by acting in this humble manner, in due time God will exalt you (1 Pet 5:6).

21. Praise and thank God
for the talents in others

We often admire the talents, gifts, abilities, and successes that God has imparted to others. However, many of us are often plagued by sadness at another's good or fortune–which is envy; or are embittered when someone has a form of a talent or gift that we also possess–which is jealousy. To be envious or jealous is to be spiritually imprisoned by ingratitude. When we are envious or jealous of others, we fall into the error of comparing, and loathing the gifts that we have received by only seeing that which we have not. A certain way to be liberated from the prison, bitterness, and resentment induced by envy and jealousy, is to thank God for those specific talents and gifts in others that incite one to be jealous or envious. By identifying those gifts in others, and praising God for those gifts in others, we give God justice, the credit due to Him for creating man in His glory. For if we are jealous of another's gifts, we are actually jealous of God and His gifts in others. When we praise God for His gifts in others, he releases us from the vexing torment of jealousy, while enabling us to become most thankful for that which He has given unto us.

22. Forgive yourself, beleiving that
God has forgiven you

The idea of forgiving oneself appears to be presumptuous, or at the very least a secular self-help mechanism that makes one feel better about himself. For how can one forgive himself of the debt that he owes God and his neighbor? Yet, Christ commands us to love our neighbor as we love ourselves, and an aspect of loving oneself is to know with certainty that those sins that God has forgiven can no longer accuse or condemn us. Therefore there is no condemnation in Jesus Christ. When a person refuses to forgive himself for an offense which God has forgiven him, he is refusing to surrender completely his past failures and sins to God. Although this has the appearance of humility, it is an attitude riddled with pride. To do so is to subconsciously believe that one's sins are beyond God's mercy. If a man has received forgiveness from Christ, he is obligated to forgive others in Christ, which demands that he forgives himself. If a man cannot overcome self-condemnation, he will most assuredly condemn others, thus incurring final condemnation. Freedom in Christ is to be graced by God with the ability to forgive others in Christ; and to forgive others in Christ, one must believe himself to be forgiven by Christ. Ongoing self-condemnation demonstrates a lack of faith in God's unfathomable mercy. This is a grave error for "without faith it is impossible to please God" (Heb 11:6).

Lord Jesus, burn the image of your holy face into me
that I may become a revelation of your glory,
that I may proclaim as did the holy Apostle:
"It is no longer I who live, but Christ who lives in me." Amen.